T0120664

Voices
IN THE
Wind

A BOOK OF VOICES IN POETRY

CARANDUS T BROWN SR.

WESTBOW
PRESS®
A DIVISION OF THOMAS NELSON
& ZONDERVAN

WestBow Press books may be ordered through booksellers or by contacting:

WestBow Press
A Division of Thomas Nelson & Zondervan
1663 Liberty Drive
Bloomington, IN 47403
www.westbowpress.com
844-714-3454

ISBN: 978-1-6642-0072-2 (sc)
ISBN: 978-1-6642-0071-5 (hc)
ISBN: 978-1-6642-0073-9 (e)

Library of Congress Control Number: 2020914151

Print information available on the last page.

WestBow Press rev. date: 08/23/2020

CONTENTS

FOREWORD

"Who is the author?" You may ask.

He is a young black man who had his share of adversities growing up in a single family.

He knew in the early stages of his childhood that he had an affinity for poems.

Living in the projects, he developed an awareness of his surroundings — both good and bad — began to put his feelings, his thoughts into the language of poems. His questions about the varieties of violence (shootings, gangs, and drug dealers) sent him in search of a spiritual belief.

The death of his nephews, a tribute to his mother and other love ones, special occasions, laudatorier to God, The birth of his first child, his marriage and a tribute to his brother who suffered a stroke, all of these among many more were set in a composition of poems.

I, his mother thank God every day that He gave this young man the wisdom to enrich our lives with his beautiful and powerful poems. I also thank you, my son, for giving me the honor of writing the Foreword to your book.

-Marva Louise Brown

DEDICATION

This book is dedicated to my wonderful family.
My wife:
Anquinetta
My Daughters:
Janae
Shayla
Jamaia
Imani
Charletta
My Son:
Carandus Jr.

God has blessed my life in so many ways that the dedication of this book is extended with love. To my Parents, siblings, relatives, and friends.

Especially to God the Father, God the Son, and God the Holy spirit. I would have never discovered the gift to express myself through writing and knowledge of inspiring words.

"THE TRUTH"

Am I ugly because of my color
Am I indecent because my skin is darker?
Do I not share the same insides as everybody else?
In your eyes, I might be nothing
In Truth's eyes, I am beauty
I am glamorous, full of wisdom and knowledge
To truth I am a key of love for everybody to share
You might see me as an old dusty book on the cover
But inside I am adventure, comedy, excitement, a thriller all in one If you
only take the chance to read me
To you, I am a problem
To Truth, I am the answer
I am the finder, the option, the problem solver
In truth we share these abilities to build a greater world
I'm more than just a cloudy gray sky
If you can look beyond that point
I'm yellow, orange, red, blue, and purple
I am a bursting rainbow with a pot of gold at the bottom.
They say that everything is left in the eyes of the beholder
WRONG!
Everything we behold is in the eyes of Truth
So, hold onto Truth and judge People by the inside and not the out.

God is our Truth in life remember Him above all
and Truth shall be displayed on to you.

1992

"THE DREAM"

Laying In bed at night, I wonder
What's wrong with my brothers and sisters
Do we wonder as a people or as a strong culture?
Why are we killing and taking our lives?
When our hearts are built with a strong foundation of love
We are not, and should not be, a dying population
In a dream out of reality, I lost a friend
I asked can we get back to growing as a loving population
Not just for us, but for the life everybody wants to live
If we are one in Christ
In Christ, we have what it takes to love each other
Through all the hurt and misunderstanding in the black community today
Be are the ones to make a difference
You see, as God placed a dream in Dr. Martin Luther King Jr's spirit
We still have dreams placed in our spirits
That nations, black, white, and brown Come together as all God's children
That we can see a world as it is in God's eyes

1992

LORD, I WONDER, AND I ASK

Oh Lord, thy Savior, why must we live in such a prejudiced world,
Where corruption seems to guide the inner soul
Where Your love is not at the top of the hearts of man,
Where one color seems to be more dominant?

Why does it appear others look down on us
Because of the mere image my skin?
Why does it seem to be like that
Being black is a harder life to live?

Why, Lord, does it appear that what others think, looks to be true?
Why do we prove the views of ignorance to be right?
Why do we, as children of The Most High God
Keep ourselves set so low down, when we come from so high?

He answered, "My son, lift your head up.
Are you not man made in my own image?
Did I not give you the same breath of life as all others?
All this was done to build a better world!
Never for an easy one to lose appreciation for what I have done."

"You are not judged, looked down on, or thought of as wrong
If you love me is the only truth you need
There is no color that I see, only my children who come to know me
The love I give to you is for you to express to those I place your way."

"There are only two types people in this world
The saved and the unsaved."
And, as He left me with His last words, "Are you saved?"

1992

"STRUGGLES"

I am a Christian and this is where I stand.
I was born again to be a Christian man.
Because my Lord says that I can.
The path I chose is not an easy one.
It's filled with traps, destruction, and drop holes.
Many misleading facts and untrue doors.
But know keeping focused on the Lord will get you through.
It is long, rough, and hard at times.
Remember the Lord will be your guide.
His light will shine your path to Him.
He will always be your guard.
When Satan comes to see that you fall.
Don't worry if you stumble, just don't even stay down.
Stand up firm and say to him.
"In the name of Jesus, I rebuke you, satan.
Cause my Lord has called me to stand with Him.
When he keeps coming back and won't give up.
Telling you he's your friend.
Let satan know, say to him, "I am a Christian".
This is where I stand.
I was born again to be a Christian man,
Cause my Lord knows that I can.

1993

"WHEN MY LORD COMES"

For when my Lord comes
There shall be a new Heaven and Earth
A new Jerusalem (The Holy City)
Peace, love, and unity, for God's people
For when my Lord comes
He shall do away with all the evil nature of man
All the people in sin traveling with it
We shall see Satan and his followers fall to their doom
For before my Lord comes
We must help those who are not saved
Share and spread the word of God
That they may not feel the wrath of God
On judgement day
The more that comes to know Him shall please Him
For when my lord comes
He shall take His children whom He loves dearly
To the place He has chosen for us
And His name we shall rejoice and praise
Live in harmony as it is promised
For when the Lord comes

1993

"I AM"

I rest in peace on Heaven and Earth.

Cause for this short time I spent it was well worth.

Give me the pain, the hurt in your heart.

For I am glorified now, and we shall never be apart.

I am like the wind; I shall carry on.

Cause from this day forth, you will never be alone.

I am blessed now, to see you one day again, in God's kingdom where we are rich as kings.

When you began to cry and your tears start to drop, I will be there to comfort you and hold your hand.

I will never leave your side because with you is where I stand.

I am up in the sky, near the ocean blue.

Wherever you are I am there to honor you.

Through the nightmares that you may have.

Think of me, the perfect dream.

Take my smile the perfect gleam.

I am your star of the night shining down.

The sun of day glowing all around.

Your love is caring, kindness, and the best you gave in being my mother. The memories of me will always be with you, so think back on me when you need a friend and I will remember you.

1995

"WHY"

Why!! Why!!
Why must we die at the hands of our own?
When a young child's mind can grow to be so strong.

Why!! Why!!
Why don't people look to you to find hope and rise above these worldly times?
We were not put here to do such devilish crimes.

Why!! Why!!
Why do I see such broken hearts?
With so many families torn apart
Young brothers and sisters left lying dead
No help came for them to get ahead.

Why!! Why!!
Why do we bring tears to our loved ones eyes?
When you have placed the love in us to break all their cries.

Why!! Why!!
Why does life pursue us to take such an easy ride?
Never truly opening our minds to you from the inside.

(Why! Why must I ask Why?)

1995

"I BELIEVE IN MIRACLES"

I believe in miracles
I see it everyday
In the stress, the hurt, the sadness, and the pain
she goes through everyday
keeping joy in her heart
Going beyond the limits to ensure her kids are okay.

I believe in miracles
I see her everyday
A knight in shining armor in her own special way
She protects us, serves us, she fights a constant battle
Never giving up, she must win the war
For she is always there with us
Doing all she can and more.

I believe in miracles
I feel her everyday
When she's not around
The strength of her love is still there
The embrace of her hugs
The power of her will to endure
The expressions of her mind
Is a depression cure

I believe in miracles
I hear her day and night
Like when she says, "I love you, no matter what happens I'll be there!
Anything is possible and always follow your dreams,
Keep looking to God in everything"
I know these are the true words she means

I believe in miracles
The way she takes her time with me
In all the things she does to go further and further
like a perfect rose she is meant to be.

What is she? My Miracle, Mother.

1995

"THE SMILE"

The smile he had he gave each one of us apart
To share, to comfort, to heal our hurting hearts
The smile he had shall forever glow through the years and days to come
Each minute there is, he will never leave us alone
The family he left, he loved so dear
If he could, I know he would wipe away our painful tears
The smile he had touched, and intensified people lives
He will always be there to sooth our mournful cries
The smile he had was loving and true
I found out the day he departed he made a prayer good-bye to me and you
The smile he had will never die
Its in our heart, mind, and soul
It's in the blink of your eye.

The smile of James Lesley Harkins III leaves an
everlasting impression that will never end
He was more than a nephew; he was my Best Friend.
February 21, 1989 – June 29, 1996

7/1/96

"WHAT WILL IT TAKE"

Shots blast, bullets racing towards me
A thought comes to my head
What will it take to stop!
This senseless violence

I didn't mean
It to end this way
If I ask what it will take
The answer would be
I wish I had just one more day

To change the words
Come back my son, come back
Momma is here
What will it take?
For my mother to not deal with her worst fear

What will it take?
I will never see my family or loved ones again
Was my path I took
Worth all this hurt and pain

What will it take?
I always figured my life was chosen for me
Is this how God meant for me to live
Or
Is it possible to let the children grow up and be!

Dreamers to lead a life away
Senseless deaths seem to grow more and more
Each day by day
What will it take?
To never go to another senseless funeral

What will it take?
To think first
On
Who this senseless violence will affect?
Not just for the families
But for God's sake

1997

"FOUNDATION FOR THE FAMILY"

He is the foundation for the family
The source that created life
He puts bread on the table
He is the binding tie to hold the family together
The seed from which hope grows
The strength in the root that keeps it firm
Order is best kept when He is around
Chaos and confusion come when He is gone
He is the guide for family values
He is the protector and guard to His family's safety
He is gentle and loving as a kitten
Or a warrior in rampage because vengeance is His
When needed to be
He makes dreams to come true
And nightmares to fade
He is the narrator of stories
Whose voice carries you off to fantasy land
He can be your best friend through joy and pain
He can be found in every man
He is the father of father's
He is the foundation that starts the family

Who is He? A God Fearing and Trusting Father

1996

"SPECIAL THANKS"

A special thanks we would like to say,
Because you have been there for us in so many ways,
Time after time, over and over again,
You have done more and more, all you can.

A special thanks we give to you,
From the bottom of our hearts for it is past due,
We are grateful for the help you gave to us,
Cause all this time you never had to.

A special thanks we engrave to you in stone,
Because you could've given up and left us on our own,
Rather you believed in us or not, it kept us strong.

A special thanks we are giving out,
For helping us to realize what we need to care about,
A special thanks from us to you,
To last forever, to be refreshed and new.

To those who have done all they can for the one's they love.
May God bless you!

1996

"WHAT CAN I CONQUER"

What can I conquer?
My fears, pain, dreams, and my life
It seems so hard to beat
I often wonder can I conquer life's defeat
Lord will I fall into my own self-defeat
What can I conquer?
Yesterday, I never thought it would be like this
Today, I fear is on my mind and wondering about the risk
What can I conquer?
The pain is always there
An empty void hovers around me, which make this life one big nightmare
What can't I conquer?
For you have delivered my victories into my hands
A heavenly family beside me
To guide me before I fall
What can I conquer?
All things, cause in You Lord, I cannot fail

1996

"MY LITTLE ONE"

My little one
How misunderstood you are
Why do you flood the world with tears?
I have not left you or moved far away
This world can be scary in the midst of your fears

My little one
I have not forgotten you
Or left you alone
Let me help
My love is never gone.

My little one
The pain you feel is only temporary
I will help you heal
If you just open up to me
And follow My will.

My little one
How I miss the smile on your face
Seeing you playing and having fun
It never left; it's still there in that one special place
Joy comes in the morning under the rising Son.

My little one
My heart is in pain to see you this way
But things will be normal again
If you put your trust in Me on this day.

1997

"I BELIEVE IN YOU"

I believe in you
And what you can do
Let nothing get in your way
Or keep you from your promised day
I believe that you can let your mind soar
As high as you want
And still continue going on for more.
I believe that you can give the world what it needs
That what you can do is like the world's tallest tree
Planted from the start of its seed
What I see in you
I know you see it to
How the greatest mind can be the strongest of clues
That everybody has but those that use it is only a chosen few
I believe that you can be whatever you want
By using your mind to understand
What you know you can do
This is why I believe in you.

1997

"IF WE COULD HAVE SAID GOODBYE"

If we could have said goodbye
The things we could have told each other
We would have done more things together.

If we could have said goodbye
We would have said how much we love you
How much we have taken more time thank you.

If we could have said goodbye
We would appreciate the small moments laughing, joking, talking
Teaching and crying, but above all healing.

If we could have said goodbye,
We would have grown closer with one another
Sharing in the last moments we had together.

So now we say our good-byes
In the way only our spirit can express
So God let it be known
A thankful goodbye for the memories left.

1997

"SHAKING TO THE GROUND"
(What satan sees, when dealing with Jesus)

How many are leaving
I can't; I won't face this doom alone
They are all rising up against me
Who is it? Tell me! Who have they found?

It is Jesus Christ their savior!
Who has put His blessing upon their life!
They have found out the truth
And now our doom is yet to come.

What is wrong satan?
Why do you tremble at the name of their Lord?

(Pause, silence, and then a sudden roar!)

We must destroy their faith
And lead their souls back to me
For I am satan! And I alone will be their only lord
And I will see that they perish here with me.

Listen to them, shouting and praising His name
Look how they follow Him and glorify His name

My followers of evil, attack, attack!
We shall put an end to their glorious Praise

(On the battlefield)

As Satan followers tried attacking us
All at once they fell to the ground
We looked around to see what had happen
When we notice our Lord Jesus,
Has Satan
"Shaking to the ground"

3/28/98

"WHEN I CALL"

My children: why do you not listen when I call
Do you not want to hear what I have to say?
Do you not want to know me?

When I call you
Why do you turn away and act as though you have never heard my voice?
Yet, I have always been with you and talked to you!

Why have you forgotten me?
From since you were born, I have held you in my arms
It was I who raised you, comforted you, played with
you, and taught you my righteous decrees!

I am the father of your fathers
The creator of all, and the leader of nations
I am the alpha and omega, the beginning and the end
Still! You do not listen for me.

I give you promises that can never be broken
Gifts that last forever, love that can never be deprived
I give you blessings beyond counting, and yet
you still do not hear me when I call.

I call that you may be delivered to me
To join me in my kingdom
So that you may receive eternal life.

My children open your ears to me
Let me heal your tormented soul
Mend your broken heart and revive your fading spirit.
So, listen for me when I call.

4/2/98

"IMAGINE"

Imagine yourself in front of a firing squad
Faced with life or death
What would you be thinking at this given time?

Imagine the orders was just given to shoot
To take your life away
What will you say?
This is the moment you have left.

Imagine the sound of the guns blasting
Bullets racing out of its barrels
Heading straight for you
Will you then cry out, "Lord save me!"
(Will He listen)

Imagine as the bullets, tearing and shredding through your body
While in seconds, time seems to be hours
What will you think as the pain is numb
Finally erupting into your body with so much suffering.

If you have always believed in God
Why then do you wait to the last minute?
To say, "Lord forgive me"

What is happening during this time?

So, did He listen?
Are your sins forgiven? (I don't know)
But if you're in heaven with me
Then we are both thankful that the Lord listens when we cry out to Him.

4/3/98

"THANKFUL"

I thank you Lord for all the wonderful people you brought into this world,
People who help build, strengthen, and love you.
Like a second family I have come to know
People that are a blessing to me beyond compare.
They help me build my life to a higher level
A point without you Lord I could never imagine
For you brought me to a church to be filled with your Spirit
Pastors, deacons, ministers, teachers, and supporters with the warmth of your care.
You brought me to a home of stability, strength, kindness, and love
To a home where you Lord are the base of their foundation
This is sometimes found to be very rare.
How I thank you Lord for a family in church and in Christ
Thank you for people that helped me to draw closer in you
A church that has showed me how to do all I can without despair.
Oh Lord thank you for showing me what I was seeking in this world of uncertainties
Lord for blessing me with such wonderful people at a time when things seemed to be at a distant glare.

4/1996

"WHERE THERE IS JESUS"

Where there is Jesus
There is the truth for a new beginning
To live in righteousness in the land He sent before you
A beginning where eternal life is promised
That His unfailing love is yours.

Where there is Jesus
There is strength in His name
To empower your spirit over the nature of the flesh
Where in Him the devil cannot prevail against you.

Where there is Jesus
There is comfort in being one with Him
Comfort that brings you light in your darkest of moments
Comfort that shields you from harm and cuddles you like a babies sleep.

Where there is Jesus
There is a commitment to us
To redeem us when we ask Him into our hearts
A commitment of death for the salvation of man

Where there is Jesus
There you can be just as well
He sits at the right hand of the father calling out to us

4/1998

"GRASP"

Grasp the light
You see right before you.
Remember me from birth you came
I have not left you alone
Come to me; hold on to me, I love you my child.

Grasp the Joy
I have given to you.
Be not broken hearted
I know your pain
Be not weary
You're not bearing what you can't handle.

Grasp the Holiness
You seek all around you.
Cause it is with the fellowship and the righteousness of other
Like you who seek to know me
That will help you to continue to grow.

Grasp my Words
So you may learn the way and the truth.
That the devil may not send you astray
And will deceive you with trickery and lies
That you may stand firm in knowing me.

Grasp my Blood
From out of me, freely given for you
Your sins can be forgiven
Eternal life can be yours
For the kingdom of heaven is to be yours.

Expressed through a vision

4/98

"OH LORD A PRAISE OF THANKS FOR YOU"

Oh Lord, you are my purpose in life, my reason for living,
I give myself to you completely, for my heart seeks
to be a righteous man of faith relying on you.

Oh Lord, you have embraced me in your arms
during my darkest moments, like an eagle soaring through
the clouds, I sit upon your wings and let my burdens
fall from me.

Oh Lord, life is meaningless without you, a constant drift
of worries never to be lifted off my shoulders,
Like a pencil without paper never to write the
full story, no words to read, no sentences to
fill in the paragraph, no phrases to draw conclusion,
no book to show expressions, life is meaningless without you.

Oh Lord, countless of times you have been there for me,
even at the times when I turned my back on you,
Now I understand the story of the protocol son
for the love you have always expressed to me in my every day life.

Oh Lord, everything I am in life is because of you,
you give me strength to my weakness,
encouragement to my follies, peace to my soul,
forgiveness to my sins, truth to the lies of the devil,
love of being with me no matter what, and
QUALITY OF BEING GENUINE THE ONLY ONE.

6/4/98

"IN FAITH"

In faith you believe without doubting
Without fear you choose what is right
Faith is the part of us that draws us closer to our Savior.

In faith what you think can't be done
Is already happening
What you can't see is already shown
What you say you can't hear is already heard
Through faith in Christ Jesus.

In faith you know that God has no limit to his love
There is nothing impossible that He can't do
There is no evil that overcomes Him
No strength that is stronger
No demon or devil to ever replace our Lord Christ Jesus.

In faith our spiritual level can't stop growing
Our need for Him in life can never fade out of awareness
Our control over our flesh will never be controlling to us
For the love of Jesus is greater.

In faith He is the ultimate love and power
For what this world throws at us
For what it tries to give us
through faith in His name, we are given much more
"The Blood of the son; Jesus Christ".

Faith is believing what is not possible
for our eyes, mind, and body
to touch, smell, and see.

6/4/98

"A REPORT IN HELL"

satan, just when we thought we had them!!!
Their Savior showed up as they called upon His name, everything did would not hinder them, they became to strong. They begin rebuking us out, the room then beamed with light, couldn't stay any longer we gave up the fight. For His name pierced through us and we were gone.

satan, we kept trying to find other ways back in, but just as we would creep the door back open, they somehow knew we were there. They SLAMMED the door back shut, as they got stronger and stronger. We got weaker and weaker there was nothing else to done.

satan! **only if we had seen it at first** ! We might have had a chance, but now they are numbered against us, all becoming more like Him, following in His steps, His ways, and finding themselves within His body and in Him they have become one.

satan, what can we do, time is getting shorter. We know what the WORD say and, in our doom, we can go no further! How can we attack them even harder, when their belief is now in Him. We have no strength or power to even face the presence of them.

satan, these are the times, we heard many of them talking about, the ones we thought we had for sure, Their faith grows in number and they now find themselves to be a force of Him, for seeing the others who already serve Him.

satan, we cannot win this fight for the **HOLY SPIRIT** is among them. They shout battle cries and their awareness is more of Him. They are starting to be transformed from our hold, conforming only to their Lord. They think and act more like the One stories were foretold. How do we get them to fall, when His anointing covers them all.

6/11/98

"HALF AND WHOLE"

Why father
Do we as a people give you half of ourselves
That we can give you that part of us
We want to give you
Then expect that you will still give us your full blessing.
Why, do we say to you Lord we will be complete to you
"When it's right or convenient for us"
But expect your love to be with us
"ALWAYS"
How is it Lord that we want your full love
But not be willing to give you the same back
If it were not for you giving us your Son
We would not be at this point of grace now.
Why is it at our worst time in life
We think we will let you know all about us
To expect that you being,
who you are that you have no other choice but to indulge in us
Why is it Lord
That we cannot just love you without the entire blessing
That you've given to us in our life
Showing us that you are real and never forsaken?

6/12/98

"HIS CRUCIFIXION"

Can you imagine what it was like at the time of His crucifixion?
To think of what was going through the minds of
His people at the time of His death.
As tears covered their eyes
In the moment he took his last breath.
Can you feel the sadness of that time?
In the moment the son of God chose to die!

Can you feel the greatness of His love?
For Him to die for you and me
The pain and the humility He endured
laugh after laugh, slash after slash.
For the sins of selfish people
That we may have a life and freedom with Him to receive.

Think about what people said and thought
When they heard Him say!
"Father forgive them for they know not what they do"
What would you say or think?
What a great man he is!
Or
Still curses Him to the grave!

After His death
Did His people know or understand?
The commitment that He had made!
An everlasting sacrifice for a people
Living selfishly with selfish ways.
A commitment to save lives
From death that limits our days.

When Jesus was crucified on that day
He touched the spirits of His people
Anointing us with the power of the Holy Ghost
When He placed in front of us the kingdom of heaven.

7/17/98

"SPIRITUAL GIFT WRAPPED"

Spiritual: Having to do with God.
Gift: A present, A sacrifice, something given at no cost.
Wrapped: To cover, envelop, and secure for transportation, or storage.

Spiritual gift-wrapped is God giving us gifts at no cost
in covering the world with His anointing.
The securing of the world in His name
for transportation of our souls in living with Him.

Spiritual gift wrapped is the sacrifice He made for us
being wrapped in His blood that He gives freely to us.
To live in His kingdom for eternity
sparing our lives on the cross for our sins.

Spiritual gift wrapped is the gift that He gives to us
that makes us better servants of His name.
Willing to find out what our gifts are
using our gifts to benefit the body of Christ.

Spiritual gift wrapped is accepting our gifts
being gifted children of God.
Knowing that we will have to give to others
the way the Father gives to his children

Spiritual gift-wrapped is how we respond to His gifts
The way we use them in return.
How we accept and respect them
By being children of **THE MOST HIGH.**
This is being spiritual gift wrapped.

7/20/98

"THINK"

Think about your kids for a second, how much you love them
how you would want them to grow up, being such loving, respectful,
well behaved kids, how being a proud parent of knowing that you've given
them every necessity to have a good life.

Think of the times you taught them the difference between right and wrong
because you would never want any misfortune too ever happen to them,
to never get caught in a situation that may cause harm to them,
or even death.

Think about how one day your kids may seem to be following in the steps
you guided them into, and the next day they **rip** your heart out, they start
running with the wrong crowd, disrespecting you and others, not caring
about where their life will end up, for not really thinking about the
consequences of their choices and the end results.

Think about the times you must face, to get them to understand you now
and the help that you try to give them, the sacrifices you will make for
them out of the love for your children.

Think about the pain and hurt you feel, the tears you have shed
and the many more yet to come, why did this happen when you gave
them all they needed and what they needed to know plus more, and giving
up might be an option, but never a possibility.

NOW THINK ABOUT ALL THAT AND THINK
HOW OUR HEAVENLY FATHER, THE ALMIGHTY
GOD MAY FEEL ABOUT US
WHEN WE WILL FULLY
FALL SHORT OF HIS
GLORY.

8/27/98

"WOMEN OF FAITH"

Oh Lord, I thank you for sending such dedicated women into our lives
Women who devote themselves to serving you over selfish pride
Women who have been touched and anointed by you
Women of faith to help God's children through

Women that are gentle, but strong,
Kind, but direct,
In every moment they acknowledge you with respect
They follow you to lead the path of lost souls
Women whose salvation relies in you that the world may know

Women that go the distance and push on the extra mile
Without focusing how much further they continue the trial
They are constantly growing, giving and
filling the emptiness of others,
With your knowledge they teach your words as a loving mother
Their blessings are heaps of mountains for their faith in you
We don't do enough to praise them in honor of you

Women who have the gift of patience in waiting on selfish people,
To help us figure out that it's you we're missing,
No matter how long it takes they stay to plant that seed
Women of faith is what we need

Who help your people to listen for Your voice and call
Women who are prayer warriors and remain steadfast through it all
Women whose main purpose is serve
That give their all for the family of God
So I ask you to let them know how much they are deserved

10/27/98

"REMEMBER THE CALL"

Remember the time when you heard the Lord call,
He called you by your name,
the name of His child who has lost their way home,
what were you doing that kept you so busy you wouldn't listen,
what was so important that it kept you in withdrawal?

A withdrawal that only your spirit knows and feels
but you discount the spirit
looking for anything and everything that this world offers
to live in sin
you've become like a drug addict never really finding that right push
trying to fill a void of emptiness
that can only be filled when you answer the Lords call.

A call to save your life
a call that reaches deep into your very soul
where the mind isn't cluttered in darkness
consumed in self-control
where you knew from birth he would call your name.

Remember that time when you heard His call
for to drop from eternal life into hell will be a heavy fall
and in hell you try to listen for His words
but
because you wouldn't listen earlier your shout of cries
will never be heard.

12/8/98

"TO BE COVERED OR NOT"

To be is to be covered in the blood of Jesus Christ
to dwell in the arms of the father
to glorify His name
to be heirs to his throne

To be is knowing that you're not an orphan
that you're a child of the almighty father
a brother and sister in Christ
a part of a heavenly family never to be left alone.

To be is overjoyed in His Glory
overpowering in His strength
overflowing in blessings, wisdom, knowledge, love, and care
overabounding to be plentiful in His name
Fading away from living knave

To be is being saved by the death of Jesus Christ
delivered from the ways of this world
Saints in the family of Christ
anointed by the spirit of God
touched by the hands of the Creator
who molded you in His image and your life He gave?

Or Not is to be a destitute, a charlatan, a servant of this world,
deceived by the liar of lies, a hermit in the land of nowhere,
an eternally burning soul, an orphan to the devil,
an unhappy, tormented, never having nothing,
never truly seeing, hearing death all around
A very ignorant, poor slob, who could have been,
but chose the path of the wicked and now
is dead for waiting to late to be.

12/9/98

"BEING THE LORD'S VALENTINE"

VALENTINE: A sweetheart or a friend.

V erify
A nointed
L ove
E ternal
N ew
T riumph
I nspiration
N oble
E stablished

For God so loved the world, He gave His one and only Son.
(John 3:16)

God will **V**erify His name according to His word
God will **A**noint your spirit with His Holy Spirit
God's **L**ove will prevail over all in your life
God is the **E**ternal God who will give you eternal life
God will make you **N**ew by the cleansing of your sin
God will **T**riumph over all demons and principalities that ascend upon you
God will be your **I**nspiration through it all
God will make you a **N**oble of His royalty by following Him
God will **E**stablish all things to be true in your faith of Him

2/4/99

"A HOLY HEALING OF SICKNESS"

In this world lives a sickness,
A sickness far worse than you can imagine
A sickness that guaranties death
Any place, anywhere, any time, and at any moment
A sickness that digs itself into your spirit
Make a home within you to live
Feeding on unforgiven sins
A sickness that corrupts your very thoughts
That leads you into disbelief, confusion, and fear
A sickness that is unbearable, detestable, and is gross to even think that
you have it
A sickness that makes you breakout, blind, deaf, and spiritual deterioration
begins to happen,
A sickness that can be with you for an eternity, unless properly forgiven
A sickness called sin
This sickness has only one cure
A cure with no side effects, lashing out, and guaranties eternal life
A cure that you can keep this sickness from ever coming back again
A cure that gives you a Holy Healing, cleansing, to your spirit
A cure that can only be found through the Blood of Christ Jesus.

Written for all who are spiritual sick and need Jesus
to touch and heal their spirits.

2/14/99

"TEACH ME"

Lord, teach me how to be humble
In my walk with you
Teach me how to praise and glorify your Name
That I may always lift up your Name.

Teach me Lord,
How to read and understand your words with an open mind
That I may behold your wondrous works
Teach me how to fill my spirit, with your knowledge, and wisdom
Teach me how to let my spirit continue to grow in you.

Lord, teach me
How to let the Holy Spirit dwell within me,
Teach me how to learn the gifts of the spirit
To hold and know within me,
Teach me how to put the Holy Spirit and gifts to use in life
For the body of Christ.

Teach me Lord
How to be a blessing unto others,
To go out in this world, where there is darkness,
Where fear of the world has lost knowledge of you,
Teach me how to bring your light into the darkness
That your word will spread it all around
In order your light will be found.

Lord, Teach me
How to remember and keep you in my life above all
That I in the flesh will not get in your way
When you call
That I will not hinder your growth in this life
For one thing
I have learned is that
I am nothing without you
My Lord.
Teach me Lord, Teach me

2/24/99

"GOD'S BILLBOARD"

A church on the move, with a fresh new beginning,
ready to serve and always willing,
renewed in its goals, to go out into the world,
and bring back His people who was once lost.

God's billboard, the church we are now,
to proclaim to the world that God is still here,
a church to advertise His name,
by going out the doors and out our way,
to save the lost at any given cost.

God's billboard is what we wear all life long,
to teach, minister, touch, give, heal, and help,
to live by His word, and under His care.

God's billboard, anointed with truth,
sent with the Holy Spirit, and a bright shiny glare,
to be seen throughout the world
As
God's billboard.

3/6/99

"ALONE"

Saturday night, I left with my friends
We arrive at a club ready to have fun
We go inside and 1hour later
In the back corner a fight breaks out and

?

Suddenly I'm all alone
The walls start to cave in, as fire builds up all around
My mind drifts in a daze trying to figure out what's going on.

Shouts, Screams, Hisses, and Cries, is all that I hear
I turn and turn to find someone, but quick
flashes of dark shadows is all I see
I'm all alone, all alone, as my soul is being covered in fear.

I look at my body; it's being consumed in flames
I yell help! Somebody help! I'm burning in flames
Is anybody here, but nobody's around, I'm all alone
Please stop, there's too much pain, too much pain!

Laughter in the background with very faint, but getting closer words
I've got you now, I've got you now; is what I hear, yet still I'm all alone
The lost sheep who wouldn't go back to His herd.

What? (As I think to myself)

Where is everybody? here I am all alone, all alone
The shouts, screams, hisses, and cries are all getting louder
And the pain is unbearable
What? What?
Just then I remembered Jesus and the things I should have done.

3/14/99

"MEN OF GOD"

Men on fire, empowered to serve,
Ready to give their all in the name of the Lord.
We go out into this world to be a light and a blessing to others,
Transforming ourselves to be more like Christ,
while sharing His love with one another.

Men of God believers of the truth,
Studying His word
To be a greater blessing for you.
Men on the move for the greater glory of God
Becoming a driven force lead by God
Increasing in numbers, overcoming worldly odds.

Men flowing in His grace
Given Him due praise,
Into our hearts for now is the coming of His days.
We lift up our hands and exalt His name,
The devil is a liar and we will not fall to his shame.

We are equipped and built up for battle
Ready to conquer
In Him victorious we reign
Cause He claims the honor.
How can we fall, who can stand against us,
Knowing there is power in the Name "Jesus" and God will keep us focused.

3/14/99

"THE EASTER EGGS"

Easter Egg: An egg that is colored with bright colors, hidden in the shadows or hard to see places.
That can only be found by the light that reveals them.

As sinners, we are like the Easter egg
since the time, Adam and Eve ate of the forbidden fruit
We became hidden from the face of God
But God's love still surrounded us in full color
That He see like an ocean of Newts
While lost children, scattered around
We hide deep from the light to be found.

Easter: The time of the death and resurrection of Christ Jesus.

God's plan to give His children a way back.
So He sent His one and only son to fulfill the missing gap
He died on the cross to bring light in the blemish
That had kept us hidden in the shadows
He chose to redeem us

Easter egg hunt: A hunt to find the other lost eggs.

So Jesus died for us and God's light eternally seen
It beamed in the shadows, revealing those in need
But it came with acceptance of the one who paid the cost
That we shine even brighter with colors of His love
To join the search for those still lost.

Happy Easter!!!!

3/21/99

"THE DEVIL IS OUT"

The devil is out and at play with God's kids.
Messing with their heads
Confusing their minds
Trying to subdue God's will
He is hiding himself in the things of this world
To steal, kill, and destroy the truth of God
But failed he has, for greater is our Lord
The devil is busy and, on the go,
Looking out for the right chance to consume us
God's children, to fall in his deadly flow
God is leading us away by the blood of the Lamb
Because where there is life
There is God's perfect plan.
The devil is out and being deceitful to our closed eyes
But God says speaking the truth will unveil the devil lies.
The devil is out and, on the battlefield,
Ready for the taken of our souls
But God has made away for us to be victorious
By living in Him completely and whole.

3/21/99

"I CAN"

I can walk in authority with Him.
I can speak in authority like Him.
I can heal in His name.
I can face my fears through Him.
I can cast out demons in faith of Him.
I can know of Him.
I can do more like Him.
I can go out and witness of Him.
I can grow more spiritual of Him.
I can love like Him.
I can give like Him.
I can always hear of Him.
I can feel Him.
I can help touch others through Him.
I can be saved from Death because of Him.
I can live within Him as He lives within me.
I can...
I can ...
In Jesus I can do all.

4/09/99

"DARKNESS"

Darkness consumes this world where the light of God is
not revealed, Darkness is the place where evil is portrayed,
Darkness is the wasteland of demon's domain.

Do you know where your kids are?
Do you know who they're with?
Do you know what they're doing?

In the darkness satan waits for the chance to talk with your kids.
To devour them with lies, consume their lives in darkness,
teach them to love the wickedness of sin
Rebellious and disobedient attitudes tend to prevail.
To steal, kill, and destroy the light of God in their life
To cover their eye's from finding there way back home.

satan wants the kids he engulfs to be left stranded and all alone
Deserted in the darkness
Picked apart one by one
But
Where satan made his mistake
Was
Underestimating the love of God.

So God made away for you to know
Where
Who
And
What your kids are doing
It's by keeping His light lit in your life
And
Live by example as He did for us.

4/20/99

— 48 —

"GIVEN A 2ND CHANCE"

Given a 2nd chance to live once again
To become the person, God has created me to be
Given a 2nd chance to explore what God has set before me
To find the open doors, God has unlocked for me.

Given a 2nd chance to be a blessing to others
God has blessed me, to teach and serve others
Given a 2nd chance to go out and share the gospel
As it was shared with me.

Given a 2nd chance to be more than this world
Through the Holy Spirit that lives within me
Given a 2nd chance to live without sin
To have power and authority over the principalities of this world.

Given the 2nd chance to express God's love
To breath it in again all throughout me
To be with my personal Lord and Savior in heaven for His sacrifice
which he gave freely unto me, If I believe

9/4/99

"A KILLER" AND "A SAVIOR"

He is what lurks in the darkness and beneath your shadow, hiding in the one place you never thought to look back.
He studies you close, every move you make he's there looking for the right moment to attack.
To steal, kill, and destroy your spirit.
Never noticing him because of your own ignorance.
While forgetting the very one who has always been your strength.
A killer who knows you, your family, and friends.
Who knows where you live and what you do day by day?
A killer whose only motive is to see God's people destroyed and burned to their grave.
Dammed into damnation with him is his only motive.
Such a killer who has no cares, no love, and no feelings.
You or anybody else, by whatsoever mean nothing to him.
A killer who seems to have every kind of arsenal available because the lies he web.
Who on his own can never defeat you and any chance of a victory he will always lose?
If the focus on The Son you live to choose.
A killer who fall frail to the name of just one man
A man who was humiliated, beaten, and even killed by the people he led.
A man, whose love has no limits nor boundaries.
Forgiveness is only to ask for it, and eternal life is a step away.
This man is the Son of God, **"Jesus Christ Our Savior"**.

10/31/99

"SINDERELLA"
My point of view

Lost in a false family of evil, deceived by the stepmother (Satan) and stepsisters (demons) and now separated from the true Father. Lost in a family that has no cares for me or anybody else, whose only motive is to steal your soul, kill your spirit, and destroy your true testimony. Lost in a family of ugliness, disaster, and devastation all around. Lost in a family that's corrupt with the evilness of the world.

Lost in a family who denies me the chance to go to the ball (Heaven). It's always "Sinderella do this, Sinderella do that" (Sins of this world). They are just scared that I will meet the Prince (Jesus) and be saved from all this turmoil (Hell) around me.

My fairy godmother (the Holy spirit) will give me the chance to go to the ball. To behold the chance of beauty and dance with the Prince in his home. I have only till midnight (the end times) to meet the Prince once and for all, the son of the King (God) and live in glory with the royal family in the presence of God and Son.

11/17/99

Based on the story "Cinderella"

"MY PRECIOUS LADY"

My precious lady for seventy-three years, you have touched our
lives Brought a smile to our face, and happiness in our sighs.
The love, joy, and care you gave us will always be kept in my heart
A special place, I know is the reason we will never be apart
I miss you, but I know its only for a little while.

My precious lady you showed me how to overcome my fears
Find strength in the lord in the moments of depressed tears
Realize the true happiness come from the Lord.
In times of hurt it was you who helped me to subdue this world
Through the hard times that came you always endured it with a smile

My precious lady you will forever be my morning star
To guide my path, a twinkle of hope in remembering who you were
Comfort to my soul, the peace in my spirit
God's joy and laughter in the days of sad times and weary
Day after day, you have given us your best
I know you are with God your body is in eternal rest.

My precious lady God has blessed me tremendously in my short time you
I have a lifetime of memories to encourage my days thinking of you
This poem does not come close to expressing what you are worth
The knowledge you taught me and helped in my spiritual growth
I miss you dearly, I wish we still had time left

From the beginning to the ending
God made you to be special
In my life as "My Precious Lady"

11/30/99

"NO COMMON PEOPLE, ONLY COMMON THINKERS"

God makes no common people
You only become a common thinker
You become less than what God has made you to be
By becoming a common thinker
A common doer, and a common person.

God has given you the ability to stretch out your mind
Be unique in the gifts He bestowed on to you
He gave you a purpose in your life to be great in this world
The strength to overcome everything you do
In Him, anything is possible
Because God makes no common people
You only become a common thinker.

A spirit full of anointing, touched by His hands
The power to tear down strong holds
Cast out demons, heal the sick, and lead His people
A gentle heart soaring across the sky to share His light
God makes no common people
You only become a common thinker.

A common person accepts what the devil offers them
Takes personal what the devil says about them
Withdraws from God because of what the devil does to them
A common person becomes a common thinker by forgetting that God
makes no common people.

12/14/99

"MAKE A DIFFERENCE"

How does one make a difference, by sharing
the love of God that's within them?
Make a difference by His strength to carry on
Make a difference by probably being the only one doing it
But knowing you're never alone.

How does one make a difference, by not given up in the midst of the rain?
Make a difference by following your dreams
Keeping hope alive from what you have to gain
Make a difference by persevering through
Whatever obstacles that may lay ahead of you
And looking to God each and every day.

How does one make a difference, by being a
leader, a teacher, and a friend?
Make a difference by leading as an example for
others to follow, instead of a life of sin.
Make a difference by teaching the knowledge
God has made you capable of learning.
Make a difference by being a friend that people
can count on, instead of always running.

How does one make a difference, by standing up
and being **Bold** for what you believe in.
Make a difference by taking action in what need to be done
See it through until the very end
Make a difference by simply believing that you can.

12/28/99

"STOP! COMFORTING THE DEVIL"

The devil is looking around watching you closely, waiting for the right
moment to erupt your walk with God. The eyes of your enemy is on you
in everything you do. He wants to discredit you as a child of God.

Do you not know that when you wake up in the morning and
you don't give praises and thanks to God, or you go through
the day without glorifying God, and even end the night without
speaking to God? That you are comforting the Devil.

You are comforting the devil, when you're to tired to go
out and share His words, to scared to witness the truth
to others, to shame to speak the name of the Lord, and
basically to pathetic to do what the Lord ask of you.

The devil gets his comfort from the little things that you won't do.
The things that make you need to check yourself and emotions.
Stop feeling sad, depressed, unworthy, and quit acting like God has
never did anything for you. That makes you comfort the devil.

1/05/00

"REDEEMING QUALITIES"

In the beginning God created man
He perfected man in His likeness
Gave man the world and qualities of Him
To rule, subdue it, and be fruitful
Till a terrible fall came upon man
That caused man to abandon God
It led men and women into a place of separation
But God created us, for His greater glory
He came upon the world as a man
And took us back from Satan holds
And with Gods qualities created within us
He redeemed us by dying for us
Redeeming qualities that His blood was shed for
To lead us back into His presence
Redeeming qualities of eternity and everlasting life
From the beginning, we were given it
Redeeming qualities to pick up our cross and follow Him
And be joined back together in His divine presence
Being one in the body of Christ
For this life, He has given us and the blessings to come after

2/09/00

"I HAVE ALWAYS KNOWN YOU"

For years, I have known you as you grew in front of my eyes
I have always been with you every step of the way
With you, I endured all you made it through
It was I who carried you
In those moments you felt like given up.

It was I who spoke to you in the stillness of the night
I reached for you, but you turned your back
I called for you many of times, but received no answer
You refused my help
Told me "you could do it on your own."

Therefore, I allowed you to venture off
To discover life for yourself, but never alone
There were times that you would ask for me
Never realizing I was already there
When I step in to help, you took credit for the work I did
I still loved you, even though you believed I was gone!

I knew what I wanted for you
From the beginning, it never changed
A minor setback on your path, a hiccup in times side
Now here I am again calling for you
I'm not given up and I will not be denied.

2/20/00

UNSHAKABLE FAITH"

A lady of God with unshakable faith
Though the ground may shake, and the skies may rumble
Stands a woman of God giving her all to help others

Her dedication and commitment to God and
His children goes without saying
She is always there to uplift, encourage, and befriend us
She is more than what words can express
She is our spiritual mother

Anointed she is, blessed by God
A woman shaped and created from God's unfailing love
She is an example for us to keep pressing on

Her strength in God is what we admire
The way she gives us her extra and hugs when we need it
love and care when we don't feel it
She helps us to find God for ourselves
We are truly and deeply blessed to have her

Unshakable faith is to stand with God through
chaotic times, without worrying and fearing
She is doughty in her pursuit to show God
Unshakable faith is what she has
Because she refuses to lay down
Her trust in God

5/5/00

"BROKEN HEARTED"

Living life with a broken heart
Torn into pieces for the lost children of God
Whose light is lit!
But dim from them being apart
Wondering how they survive
When the devil is tempting them
With deceit and traitorous lies
With their eyes covered which makes them blind
They are slowly dying ending their lives
A broken heart split into two
On one, half there is care to help open their minds
The other despair for what they leave uncovered
The choice to live for God, or fall from the truth
Wondering if they truly know
That God is looking for them
As a worried parent does
But instead of them coming home
They live with His foe
And will never even know
When it's all over and done
I hope to feel my heart healing
With His children coming home
And the lost down to none!

5/7/00

"MOTHERS"

God's gift to the children born into this world
Delicate as a flower, gentle as a feather
They are created from God's loving heart
Placed here to be our nurturing guardian
Mother's
They give their last
To overcome many obstacles
To watch over their children with love and care
Mother's
Without hesitation they step up
To keep their families safe
They make strides to hold their family together
They press on through many days of hard work
Their days are never ending
Cuz at home their hard work is all the same
Mother's
They days of peace and quiet are few to none
One day is not enough to express the honor for our mother
Still she humbles herself and accepts this Mother's Day

Happy Mothers Day!

5/13/00

"LEGACY OF A MAN"

The legacy of a man is to be great
The example of Jesus molding our fate
What makes a man destined to be great
Is the way he lives for the Lord
To touches the hearts of others
The last impression he leaves behind!
A great man's destiny is measured by how he rises from his mistakes
The way he allows the Lord to use his mind!
The legacy of a man is to be great
He understands in difficult times upon the Lord he learns to wait
A man becomes great through his walk with the Lord
Through an endless effort to see God's will in this world done!
A man's legacy is shown by how his family stays together after he's gone
How they allow his memory to be carried on
A man becomes truly great
He chooses to pick up his cross on the war front!
He endures life's overwhelming pleasures of the hunt!
When the fury of life chases him down
His strength is in Jesus and the expressions of his heart!
The legacy of man is to be great
Therefore, God sets him apart!

Written By
Carandus T Brown
6/1/00

"BE BLESSED"

May
God bless you in so many ways
For all the help that you gave
May
Your blessings overflow the rest of your days
May
Each new venture you take
Be prosperous in the ones you make
Blessed are the lives that you have touched
In making friends God bestows much
May
Your blessings never end
That your joy will bring comfort to your friends
May
God continue to shine his unfailing love on you
To be blessed in everything that you do
May
You find His grace
Wherever you go
In the hearts of people
And so much more.

BE BLESSED UNDER GOD!!!

6/26/00

"WHAT IS THE TRUTH"

What is the truth?
That lay before your eyes
That dwells inside the dormant mind
Which by opening up the unseeing eyes
Will allow you to figure out the truth that is in disguise.

What is the truth?
Is it what you think that maybe fact?
Or is it what your senses touch, feel, sight, hear, or smell that makes you react
Or could it actually be what the mind lacks.

What is the truth?
Is it in the knowledge that you gain
Or is it in the books you read that keeps you sane
Or could the truth be from setting free your carnal mind
To a state of realization of what it can't maintain.

What really is the Truth?
It's not really the point of your hand
But the truth is when you come to know that you are just a mere man
And we can never understand God's divine plan.

8/10/00

"BEAUTIFUL"

Beauty is not about the outer appearance
Or the way you look
But a combination of your qualities
that glows through you
One is beautiful by how
They treat, love, and respect others
Beauty is what beauty does
To truly be beautiful
You must allow the best of yourself
To transcend on others
Beauty is helping others with a smile
During your time of hurt
It is to look within yourself
To find the happiness of the heart
True beauty is not capable of being selfish
But rather shared through the desires of all
Beauty is not transparent in the natural mirror
But the mirror of the spirits it can be seen
To be beautiful is a normal reaction
Without reacting out of carnal beauty
Outer beauty is but a mere glance
To inner soul
When it's not corrupted by the lust of the mind
One does not see the beauty in just the seed
But from the growing of the flower that you perceive
The measure of beauty overcomes your natural form
To a state that is truly beautiful when it is fully-grown
At that, time the perceptions of beauty will be laid to rest
That the true beauty in us all can be seen at last.

8/17/00

"TORMENTED SOULS"

Tormented souls driven by evil
Shaped into a deadly mold
Hurting within the inner fold
Lies their tormented soul
Tormented souls ridiculed and belittle by Satan's hold
Too scared to step out and be bold
Because of their tormented souls
Pain and strife are ending their lives
Becoming older and older
More colder and colder
Sustaining a heart of coal
Surrounded by a tormented soul
Tormented souls lacking in faith ready to be sold
Giving up on the true one
Who brings them hope and streets paved of gold?
Who brings peace and comfort to their tormented souls?
Lord, I need You to forgive me of the debts I owe.

10/01/00

"LIVING WITHIN"

Living within you had me fooled
Spinning in your web using us as your tool
Leading us into doom
Spreading wickedness throughout the room
Living within plotting and scheming
Destroying our lives while we are still dreaming
Tonight, my eyes are opened to your hideous face
As you move around freely in this place
I can see you, smell you, feel you, and hear the slithers of your tongue
And now your deception is sprung
Living within you thought you had won
But see I poured my heart out to God this
morning and now you will be shunned
I know what you are now and your true name
(Kabazzyism); I am done playing this game
Your hold on my family and my life is over, you're through
I plead the blood of Jesus over us, which puts an end to you
And through the passing days we will rise up
and take back the years you stole
So, go back to hell and tell Satan and others, what I now behold
The power of God and foreseeing eyes
A revelation to everything you do in disguise
Living within
Never again!

10/17/00

"WHAT YOU MEAN TO
SO MANY PEOPLE"

Sometimes it is hard for people to express what they feel
The words are there but fall still
How much you mean to them
We need the qualities you have of Him (Jesus)
The people of God would lack if there were no you
Dying on the cross in a sign that love is displayed thru
To teach us what we need to know
In our walk with God, you helped us to grow
A man of strong with sincere faith in the Lord
Moreover, the hearts you've touched will be seen all over the world
God has anointed and appointed you to go into the places that's dark
Shine your light to those that are marked
What you mean words can not compare
Nevertheless, what God has given to you, you've shown the example for us
how to share
For years you have been there for those in need
Our lives are blessed from the planting of your seed
Spiritually we will all be connected to you for the rest our days
That God has blessed us through you in so many ways.

10/18/00

"LEAD ME"

Lead me to my Promise
Let your guided light surround me
To peace, calmness, and honesty
That I may live to be free in you
To a place of shelter
Lead me to that better place
Where I can live in your grace
I see the guided light surrounding you
Our moment has come our time is finally due
Lead me to a world of love
In perfect vision, moving through and through
Now our future is overcoming our devastating past
Rightfully restoring us back to Kings and Queens
To live free at last.

2/27/01

"THE INSIGHT OF A DREAM"

To see or not to see
To believe in the vision that's later to be
Immortality is my dream of a reality that was meant for you and me
Put together by the quest of Three
Nevermore bleeding by the wounds of this world
Death is now just the desperate thought of the old world
I am saddened by those left behind wounded through satan's hold
Left to be devoured by the jaws of his hungry lies
That the flesh shall have us to believe
As the soul pleads and cries
Set in the paradox of a different dimension
While demons wait for you in the dark of evil spaces
We are giving the choice for God's redemption
Liars lurking and lying in your face
That God is lost to us through the world we choose to honor
A world changing drastically to please the measure of others
I can see the dream's light shining deep in the corner
That in the bliss of God brings hope for a brighter future
That leads me to see or not to see
That is the focus God has laid out for me.

2/27/01

"I SEARCHED"

I searched and found
That my intentions were not fully sound
I searched my thoughts
To perceive how I was at fault
In a lie that was not meant to hurt
I apologies for the image I gave you
That my intentions were misleading and untrue
Sometimes what we try to do right turns out to be so wrong
I see my fault and I hate it took this long
A friendship that may have grew to be so much more
I would redo it over, and move back to a point of before
Only time will tell what lay ahead
But someday maybe understand I didn't mean to make you mad
I searched and seen that sometimes we need more to help us heal
I hope you believe this apology, one day to be real.

03/05/2001

"IN A GLIMPSE OF AN EYE"

In a glimpse of an eye
I have seen the world cry
People on their knees waiting for the chance to live
Broken moments of cracks in hopeful dreams
Living life in death from needing help that's never seen
Visions Gone
While at the bridge of doom from being left alone
In a glimpse of an eye
I have seen people's universe crumble
To the will of selfishness that causes people to stumble
A love lacked world falling into the pit of a black whole
Slowly crying out is the spiritual soul
The need for God to revive their life and their love
That together we may grow and live to serve.

3/05/01

"EVEN A MAN CAN CRY"

I felt a tremendous hurt in the past
I been close to death and thought I wouldn't last
I have seen destruction paved in front of my eyes
By cold heartless people, living in lies
I have seen lives taken in so many ways
Children being beaten and that's they normal day
I have heard out loud the last few beats of a dying heart
Felt the sorrows of families being torn apart
Through it all, I have never cried, till the day Jesus entered my life
Took away my sins, burdens, and strife
I cried and I cried, to feel the emptiness in my soul filled with hope
To have faith in the Lord, someone at that time I didn't even know
I felt love over hurt
I've seen life being revived from death
Destruction being undone
Cold heartless people sharing care
Lives being saved
Children smiling from being loved
A dying heart, beats strongly again
Families moral and values being restored through Christ
So, I cried and cried to feel the change Christ has placed in my life
And that day I knew that even a man could cry.

3/15/01

"APPRECIATED"

Through the years we've known each other, you've been
My Guide, teacher, my spiritual leader
The best in you, have brought out the best in me
And my appreciation for you is beyond compare
The changes I've made to be better I owe to you
Through the years we spent together I learned to appreciate you
Knowledge I gained in life to live free
Is what you bestowed in me
And my appreciation is for all that you do
God has gifted you the ability to love all
Strengthening me to stand and walk tall, instead of fall
I appreciate you because you shared that special emotion from the heart
Loving me like your own and being like another
father, instead of letting me fall apart
Now that I am all grown, we remand friends with a strong bond
That's the fact that you never left me alone
And I want to show you appreciation, for all that you do!

3/19/01

"THE LOVE FOR LIFE"

I live life to be loved, and I love life to live
My life thrive off the joy and happiness of the spirit
To belong in life, be directly with one as Christ
To be lifted high, from birth I was born with a star in my eye
Gifted with gifts to touch one's soul
Sharing a smile, a helping hand, and a healing heart to make a friend
Driven with a purpose, to spread the love of God by teaching his words
that we may live
The truth in life is divine and divine is his light that guides you to believe
To realize that God is bigger than you and me
It was He that created the way for us to live free
Therefore, I live life to be loved and I love life to live more abundantly
Assuredly, Christ is the love for life I live.

3/21/01

"THE FAMILY OF GOD"

On the brink of dawn lies the foundation for the greatest family
Created with love, power, strength, and truth
Held together by (Abba) Father, God himself
Calling, waiting, looking, listening, and searching for us to return home
The family of God driven away from each other for our own selfish desires
Never gaining, just wasting in impurity, idolization, and the sinful nature
Scared from the enemy, beating us down
from what's not seen in our eyes
And still He wants His children back as a family again
Forgiving us for all that we have done
Undying love
To heal our broken spirits, mend our heart, and redeem our soul
Never failing, nor forsaken to give up on us, to quit
One family returning back to its roots
The nourishment from the seed we grow
To be the greatest family in the nation
The family of God, forever, forever and ever more.

3/25/01

"HATRED"

A disease of the mind
Breathing in the flesh
Devouring all peaceful thoughts
Living free to wreck
Hating the worse in you
That feeds the rage of anger
Displayed onto others
Fresh blows
Cycles
Every second
From the fuel of this world
That you perceive to indulge in
That flame up the hatred of self in you
Crying in rage, living in a daze
From that one place in you
That you try to keep in the dark
Running and hiding
Scared that the truth will be revealed
That hatred lives on you
Introducing it's self every chance it gets
Growing stronger and stronger
Till that moment, which His unfailing love in portrayed in your life
And
Hatred is No Longer

3/26/01

"LOVE FAILS"

Love fails when you're not receiving it
It turns from you, like dust in the darkness of a pit
You wake up and realize what you had is gone
And your heart burns, to know that the love is done
It eats away at you when reality first bites
Love fails when you have more than one strike
Never really knowing was this one true
Stricken down by a plaque that could kill you
Where do you go, when you are consumed with bitter love?
Broken spirit mourns, in search of the lonesome dove
Love hurts, when attention lacks, and it blows up from being scorned
Love fails when it is not shared in return
It's explosive when mistreated and done wrong
Love will die when it is being stepped all over on
Taken advantage of it will fade into a spilt will
To the death it will drag you, and take you through a slow kill
Love fails when this is how you feel.

3/29/01

"GOD BLESS THE CHILD"

God bless this child to dwell in your arms
That she may abide in your love away from evils harm
Lift her in your unfailing love to a place of grace
God bless this child to see the presence of your face
And as we mourn
Help us to remember her from when she was born
God bless this child no matter how she left this world
Let your judgement count from her heart as your blessed little girl
Guide her soul from this world to your side to
be in the presence of Jesus Christ
And let it be known that she did not give up on your fight
God bless this child for she lived to know you
And in her heart, you lived, where all is true
In one moment, she felt all alone and all seemed to fade
But we thank you Lord for being with her as her last breath was made
Now our trust and faith is in You
Praying and speaking out loud
Lord, all we ask is that you bless this child.

3/30/01

"CLEANSED"

Jesus, Jesus
Oh Lord
Jesus
The filth, the dirt, and the sins of my past has been washed away
A second chance given with a brand-new day
Jesus, Jesus
You have cleansed me
Took me back with redemption and set my soul free
Shackles broken for the life I used to live
Serving Jesus
You I commit myself
To you I give
Jesus, Jesus
For you loved me so
And now that I have found you
I want you even more
Cleansed by your blood
Raised up spotless from this worldly mud
Jesus, Jesus
There is no more pain
It's your love in me that makes my spirit sang
As your heavenly melodies rain down on me
I thank You
To be blessed and set free.

4/5/01

"LITTLE PEOPLE"

Little people
They pave the way to the future world
Young and energetic while their feet barley on the soil
Delicate minds searching for guidance through confusion
Smiles of joy, eyes for learning, ready to start choosing
The right path for life guided by us
They stand around through all sorts of weather to
begin their day waiting for the bright yellow bus
Little people
They are the fulfillment for a better future
They are the completion to chaos, if properly nurtured
Their lives should be safe and secured
Their minds should never be scolded or ridiculed
Mistakes will be a given
But that's all a part of growing and living
To all the kids, we are their needles
We thread their lives to their future as example for all little people

9/03/2001

HURTFUL

Have you ever seen a tear drop fall?
From the face of a person hiding behind a problem wall
To see the hurt in their eyes
To see the pain they place in disguise
Emotions formed from scares of the past
Thoughts drowned of how long it will last
Do you know how it feels to have your innocence corrupted?
To be humiliated and insulted
How hurtful it is to be all-alone
Being the only one you can count on
To open yourself up just to be crushed by broken promises and lies
To be dead on the inside from having the feeling to just die
To feel black as night from no love or care
That your problems are just too heavy to bare
Now you know how hurtful it is to see tears fall
From a person hiding behind a problem wall.

9/12/01

"WE DIED"

One Memory that will always last is
We died together
We died strong
We died in the arms of the Almighty One
We died sharing our lives
We died thinking you
We died caring
We died with the memory of loving you
We died praying in this place
Helping and saving
We died, touched by the courage of others
We died Americans
We died in such a hateful tragedy
And
Through it all
We died watching the world come together with tremendous love
We died kissing and hugging you good-bye
Yet, we live in triumph
God Bless Everyone
America, The World and All.

9/20/01

"I'M NOT AFRAID TO WALK"

Lord, from the day I was born, you held me in your arms
The first minute I opened my eyes, I began to learn
It was always you there by my side, you never left
It was your comfort, love, and care that I felt
Now I am at a point, that I must learn to crawl
I don't want you to put me down I'm scared, what if I fall

You allowed me to move a little bit with you on my own
I'm still a little baby I don't know my way around this home
Now it's time for me to take a couple steps
I'm afraid to walk on my own, I'm not ready yet, I still need your help

Pick me back up and keep me in the safety of your arms
Your comfort I miss, I'm not ready for Satan's harm
I'm afraid to walk on my own
I'm afraid to take a step; you might leave me alone

You encourage me
By letting know it will be OK!
Lord am I ready
Oh, I hope, Lord I pray!

I stand to my feet, wobbling and shaking at the knees
Fear is here, but I see your arms ready to embrace me
I take a step and fall and hit the floor
Now for some reason seeing your arms stretched out
I'm not afraid to walk
I will get right back up and take even more

9/29/01

"A ROSE BECAME OF YOU"

Over the year's people change
some for the worse and some for the best
Who would have thought?
who would have guessed?
That thorns of a rose were how you was set
At the time we first met
Growing in your own unique way
Blooming to perfection still to this day
Turning out to be a beautiful rose
Growing deep in the winter and continuing to show
That whatever you were like in the past
A rose can still grow to last
No matter how hard life was
you blossomed so true
To start from a bud with thorns
A rose still became of you.

12/22/01

"IN PERFECTION TO LIVE FOR GOD"

In perfection to live for God
She is driven
Dedicated
Committed
And a inspiration to others
A valuable leader
Courageous woman
Generous friend
And loving mother
In the years to this day
God has granted his children
Another helpful way
To learn of the lord
As a light in you
To light up new
Old and beginning candles
Taught in the truth
A special woman
That I call mom
I would like to say
Thanks
For all, that you have done.

1/1/02

"THE CHALLENGE"

You accepted the challenge that was placed before you
Overcame many obstacles
The devil set in your way
You allowed your faith in God
To bring you to this day
You have encouraged others
That was watching to follow their dreams
That achieving their goals is not impossible
Reality does not have to be what it seems
A young black man that accomplished much
Through all the odds
When many of us fall short
To live in the moment with a loud voice
That lays a path to destiny
That God has granted us through choice
So on this day of graduation
We are pleased to share it with you
Through the prays and blessing that are bestowed on you
From all our hearts
We want to say
"We are so very proud of you!"
Continue to achieve whatever challenge may come your way

2/16/2002

"FOR ALL THAT YOU ARE"

For all that you are
For all that you did
For being one of the greatest men too ever live
For taking us in
As if we were your own
And with all of us you created a home
How can we thank you, for all that you've done?
For being your best, numeral uno, **#1**
We have come to know you
From past days of joy
A feeling we treasure and hold true
For all that you are
And who we grew to be
In our eyes you are as close to perfection as we can see
For all that you did in raising us **Three.**

7/16/2002

"GREATNESS"

You see greatness defines us as a people
Rising high and seen like a cross on a steeple
Through many years of torture, we overcame
While in our hearts love and peace we maintained
That remaining together and not divided is how we kept our sane
We built our strengths from one another
Protecting our sisters and helping our brothers
Greatness flows through our bloodline
That even to this day our greatness continues to shine
Money didn't define how our hearts grew
Without even a penny our faith in God carried us through
With our strong black hands, we held our own
One close family we were never alone
Past, present, and future greatness is always there
It's in the color of our skin the greatness we bare.

9/21/02

"MY TRUEST NIG"

Words to my truest nig
12 years now
We've been the best of friends
Through thick and thin
And the craziest times
Gone to soon
You've had my back
As my ace boon-coon
From little youngster
Growing up on the streets
We were ready for anything
This world dished out at our feet
My truest nig
From the 1st day we played football
We've been tight
From the days of Crazy Horse
To putting the Mack on girls at night
From discussions of religion
To fathers growing old
It helped to grow strong in choosing God as my decision
From young CVL's
To the best man at my wedding
My brother in deed
We grew strong and steady
That still to this day
I can count on you
To always been real
In everything you did
My truest nig, the real deal

I hope you know I will always appreciate you
Plenty of Thanks and blessings in your life
I pray to hold true
Words To my truest nig
My brother I miss you!!!

12/08/02

"THIS LIFE I LIVE"

Sometimes I sit and wonder
About this life I live
Will it ever get better?
Will I survive the weather?
Or
Will it get the best of me?
I try to live righteously
Hardship dwells through it all
Sometimes tears began to fall
There's no one to blame for the choices I choose
But
Still life is hard when you're born to loose
No silver spoon was ever put in my mouth
I grew up in a money less drought
As
Hell waits patiently for me to slip
Through life on the streets, the life that I grip
Inner smiles never show a dime a dozen
But
Peace with myself is what I've chosen
Time is now my only friend
Start fresh, born again
I am ready
Lord
Guide me steady
In this life I live

2/25/03

"THE PRETTY LITTLE GIRL"

Sixteen years
It took her to learn her fears
She was ridiculed by family and friends
Treated like trash and that she became
At least to herself that is
Ashamed of the things she did
She tried to hide her face in the crowd
To keep her pain from showing so loud
Her thoughts were lost in a twisted view of reality
That began as a little girl who felt she wasn't pretty
To her life was never fair
Mentally she thought no one even cared
If she live or die
The anguish she felt made her weep and cry
She never felt love from someone who meant it
Until that day she had a heavenly visit
Her life began to shift
Surprised! she was that the Lord offered her a gift
That changed her world
The day she became
The pretty little girl

3/09/03

"LORD A PRAYER FOR MY FAMILY"

Lord, here my prayer
As I look back
On the days of yesterday
Growing up with my family
The times we spent together
Playing and laughing
I learned the truest bond of friendship through family
In my years as a child
From the adults in my family
Who showed us what family was all about?
From grandfathers to grandmothers
Aunts and Uncles
Brothers and Sisters with plenty of cousins
Through hard times of trying to get together
Somehow, we made it
We never gave up
The importance of family was bestowed in us
Through past generations we learned
We never forgot what our ancestors taught
That in slavery a family is all we have
I hope that my kids would see in us
A love of completeness
That our family will get together even more
And never lose the best part of us
The family!

4/17/03

"JOURNEY"

Take a journey through my mind
Come see the world through my eyes
The way people live and die
How pain feel from the tears I cry
That reality shows money makes the world go round
Either you have it or you get tore down
Phony smiles of people in your face
Lurk hidden desires to be embraced
Things that happen in my world make people run away
Nobody to help we just live it day by day
The most unseen madness comes from what I know
Surviving each day devastating blows
I realize I have the choice to change my view
That this reality doesn't have to be my truth
Then the journey begins to change from my mind to you

5/20/03

"WORDS"

Most people never really teach the truth
That words do have the power to kill you
Words create and shape the minds
They are the instruments to the soul of mankind
Rather you decide to love or hate
Words have the power to build or break
How we feel has a lot to do with what we hear
That there are some words we all fear
God gave words to us because they impale our spirit
It cuts deep within us no matter how we deal with it
Words deliver us the way fate guides us
The end point is that words helped define us
Bad or good we should teach the truth
That words can leave a tremendous impression in you!

5/29/03

"A FATHER'S CRY"

You are the pure enjoyment of my life
What I clinch to in the middle of the night
My world has never been the same
Since the day you all were born
My love is stronger now
That my heart has grew
It brings tears to my eyes
To think of my babies
My son and four young ladies
My special pride
Brings a smile upon my face
I would give you the world
To see you glow brighter
Every moment we spend together
The delight is mine
To see my young adorable girls
Becoming beautiful ladies
A son that's every image of me
Creating his own manhood
Every day I find a new emotion
That express how I feel
In a father's cry

Written By
Carandus T Brown
2/08/04

"TO FIND YOU"

I hear you
When you wake me
I feel you
When you touch me
I see you
All around me
Your love consumes me
Every second of the day
Without you I forget my purpose
My reason for living
My spirit drifts
Amongst dry bones
My salvation withers
Towards the gates of hell
I forgot my way
Since I left your presence
Now I'm searching
Through my own created darkness
To find you
With blind eyes
I want to see you again
With deaf ears
I want to hear you again
Without the sense of touch
I want to feel you again

Written By
Carandus T Brown
2/09/04

"THE ONLY FRIEND I REALLY KNOW"

You're the only friend I really know
Yet our friendship doesn't show
Through me that is
Trapped in a world of lies
I refused to give you a try
And I forgot about you the most High
Now I'm hurting on the inside
Wondering why I haven't died
Still living in the flesh
Waking up a broken wretch
Lost and decayed
While you began to fade
Out of my life
Now I'm left in strife
Still you're the only friend I really know
And with you by my side I can grow

4/24/04

"SINS FORGIVED"

So far it's been a short life I lived
A life full of sin
That I can't forgive
I tried my best and gave my all
Every time I would rise
I would slip again and fall
Like an addict, sin has me hooked
It controls my fate
It writes my life in its book
Yet, I still hope and pray
That I can live free
To guide my own life one day
Away from the hold of sin
To live with Christ
A life of being born again
Through the pain of angels tears
And the love of God
I will conquer my fears
To strive to live
That myself I can forgive

8/01/04

"DARKEST MOMENT"

Lord during my darkest moment
You brought me light
When I was broken down
You kept me in the fight
At the moment I hit bottom
I had nothing else
For months and years I doubted you
Yet, you stayed in my life so true
You kept me from nothing
By providing my needs
You searched my heart
And found a seed
To rise again
By my side I found my friend
When life had nothing but pain
You showed me my life I could regain
With shallow tears in my eyes
You held me and allowed me to cry
That during my darkest moment
You shined for me

8/06/04

"LIFE TRICKY MAZE"

This world has me lost and trippin
Mind baffled from constantly slippin
I feel like I'm dead and gone
From to many things ending up wrong
I grew up never able to gain
Every day it begins to rain
I manage though from the sweat of my hands
Somehow, I found a way to stand
Breaking down my fears
Shedding a few tears
I wanted to press on
Like an abandoned child I found strength by my own
Trials and tribulations delivering its test
I failed quite a few, to now ace the rest
Every new page in my life I would write
Ended up in another fight
Now weary and dazed
My eyes burn more while my heart is set ablaze
To conquer life's tricky maze

8/15/04

"YOU RESCUED ME"

Lost in destruction
Trapped in the flesh
Bound to death
The beast in my belly
Lived in me
Till the day you set me free
You rescued me
You cried for me
You even gave your life for me
I feel the pain being lifted from me
I feel like shouting
I feel like crying
I feel your love placed in me
The day you set me free
You rescued me
You cried for me
The day you died for me
You took away the void
That wallowed inside of me
That nearly killed me
When the beast lived in me
You came and rescued me
By dying to SAVE ME!!

8/23/04

"YOU"

Since the day I 1st met you
My life has never been the same
Mentally I'm consumed with you
Spiritually drawn to you
Physically lost in you
Intrigued to know you
What is it about you
That placed a hold on me
That dwells through me
Unconsciously drowns me
Your beauty appeals to me
Your smile impels me
That has caught me
I find myself thinking
Dreaming
Wishing
And praying
For the chance to show you
That I just want to be real with you

9/30/04

"HOW I FEEL"

I don't know what it is
I can't explain how I feel
It's like being reborn
All over again
I'm falling deep
Deep for you
Weak in the knees
Hard to breath
I want to be everything
You ever dreamed
Give you the world
In the palm of your hand
Right beside you
I would stand
Be the love that you mentioned
The one that never ended
I still don't know what it is
But I guess this explains
How I feel

9/30/04

"I FOUND A MOMENT"

I found a moment
Where I was lost in you
Wanting to find out everything about you
We had a night that passed my dreams
Now every minute I start to Fein
Thinking of you drowns my thought
Has me scared to find out your own fault
To explain what I feel
Simply put I'm intrigued of
Your look
To your touch
To your style
That makes me go wild
Instantly hooked
I was lost in you

9/30/04

"KNOWING YOU"

I never knew how much you cared
I never knew all that you shared
I never truly knew your love wouldn't fail
I never knew it was you on the cross they nailed
I lived life without knowing you
I covered my eyes and ears from the truth
So, I ran and ran
Afraid to become the man
You created me to be
I never knew how far your arms would stretch
To bring home a sinful wretch
I never knew how much your forgiveness overflowed
Till the day Christ in me arose
That the sinful wretch died in me
I became the man you created me to be
I knew that moment your love would never fail
That you cared enough to keep me from hell
By sending your son to be nailed to a cross
That I might be saved from a life that's lost
Now my eyes and ears are uncovered to the truth
That I can live freely in knowing you

11/10/04

"IN THE PAST MONTH"

In the past month
I've discovered myself
I searched my soul and found nothing left
See I was empty inside
From trying to hide
My feelings for you
So I'm breaking down to tell you the truth
That I found a new world in talking with you
And at this point if I turned back I could be lost without you
You have built a bridge from my heart to my soul
You have created within me an everlasting smile which has me whole
In the past month
I discovered that I can breathe again
The scars of the past have begun to mend
I have opened my eyes
To see that it's you I realize
Surrounding my dreams
You are the vision I seen
From my childhood past
To be reoccurring so fast
Restarting life to make this the last
No more wallowing in my fears
However this ends up I'm hoping it's together for the rest of our years
That on this New Year "Most Loved" will be my reality
In "Knowing the Woman Behind the Name" Queenie
I had a talk with God
That has this feeling so odd
That I am blessed with a piece of his Great love
In a second chance with you God's blessing from above

11/11/04

"BOOK OF MY LIFE"

I wonder if a man can speak his true feelings
Or
Do I keep the surface of my sub-feelings?
The book of my life
Written is my sin and strife
Through the pages I turn
Allows me to watch and learn
I look back on my past mistakes
To discover this pattern of failure
Is mine to break
That on my knees
I'm praying Lord please
Help me understand
What it means to be a man
You see I have five little ones counting on me
I'm lacking who they need me to be
If I can speak what I truly want to say
I admit I cannot do it my way
I apologize that I have lost
A broken soul spent at any cost
I'm paying for my mistakes more as time goes by
My spirit laid waste to die
It's hard waiting on you to arrive
Every moment that goes by becomes harder to survive
But I am here I am still alive
Allow me to forgive my past
To give you the page to finish the last
To rise again and be my best
To speak and become that man to pass the test
That in every new page I can follow what you write
That my book will never leave out of your sight

1/01/05

"INSPIRED"

Here's what you think inspires me
The violence you portray of us on TV
The black on black crime you want the world to see
Finding a liquor store every 2 to 3 miles
All the court cases of blacks on trail
The black men beaten, killed, or thrown into prison
The laws put together to justify an ungodly reason
Inspired by all the churches that won't get along
While the body of Christ is left undone
The bad hype placed on our lives today
To build an image, but hiding in the shadows far away
The warped view of how our reality began
The truth remains we struggle each day just to make ends
Naaa... Here's what inspires me
The way blacks pull together through adversity
The way the black heart continues to grow
From all years of corrupt knowledge in history we know
Through all the turmoil we had to put up with
Our spirits never broke we refused to quit
The way we overcame every obstacle threw at us
From what we see in the media our people we still trust
The way God covers us with his hands
That through the struggle we can lift our heads and stand
I am inspired by all that we do
Cause I understand the struggles we continue to grow through
And we forgive tirelessly in hopes of starting new

1/20/05

"KNOW THAT I WILL ALWAYS LOVE YOU"

JANAE my first born
The one I adore
Who helps me breath even more?
You share my living heart
Our beat will never be apart
SHAYLA the sparkle of my eye
The tears of joy I cry
You're the smile that refuses to frown
The reason my world keeps spinning around
CARANDUS my only son
My special one
Completeness of me
The one who drives me
JAMAIA my light
Who gives me sight?
The one who gives me her unfailing love
God's gift from above
IMANI my funny girl
The brightness in my world
The one that brings laughter to my days
The reason I pray
CHARLETTA gifted and special
AKA Charles, my heart forever
You have intensified my life with deep emotions
That like my OWN it's a proud devotion
Know that I will always love you all
Together my life remains true to you ALL

1/05/05
Revised. 07/20/2012

"UNNECESSARY SCARS"

To my mother
I apologies that it took me almost 30 years
To let go of my anger and my fears
To find out the son I was
How I disrespected and disregarded who you were
I still don't really understand
But now my eyes are opening to God's greatest plan
He's helping me to become a man
You see I had a hate for you
By not paying attention to all that you been through
That led me to a talk with my sis one night
She explained something's that God told me was right
I excluded myself out of my family
Confused thoughts took hold of me
I grew up blaming you for the things I was doing
Because I allowed the devil to bring my love for you to a ruin
As hard as this is to admit that I'm wrong
I apologize that it took so long
Blinded from all the time that I hid
I now realize the truth in all the things you did
In raising us as a single mom on your own
Caring for 4 kids to have a home
You never gave up on me you reached out even further
God told me to be proud of you as my mother
With dry tears in my eyes
I sit here thinking of what I put you through with a remorseful cry
I want you to know that I thank God for who you are
And I apologize for leaving you with unnecessary scars

1/06/05

"POVERTY"

Poverty a plaque that rides us all
A disease that will be our fall
Black, White, Tan, or brown
It doesn't care through who it moves around
Born into it and...um
Through death it continues to carry on
From generation to generation
Sometimes it might jump the gap
But eventually it finds its way back
Through bad choices and lots of mistakes
Poverty the people killer if dealt with to late
Through years we may learn to survive
But... In the end it still corrupted so many lives
Just for the chance to beat it or make it out
Laziness is what it's all about
Fear is how it keeps you down
Accomplishing your goals is how you break it down

01/15/2005

"A WALK TO REDEMPTION"

Wake up my child
Take a walk with me
Share a conversation with me
Tell me what troubles you
That keeps you distant from me
Why do you pass judgment upon your life
Condemning yourself
I know your heart
I forgive your sins
I created you for your moment
That the devil is trying to steal
Your troubles are my tears
It pains me that you do not know that I am already here
You act as if my love is gone
That I can't redeem you from the things you have done
I asked you to walk with me
Put away yourself and follow me
Be who I created you to be
Your burdens I will carry
If you redeem your faith in me

2/03/05

"IN MY WORLD"

Sometimes we find strengths within our own struggle
When there's no one left to believe in us
In my world I was left to fend on my own
A world that I was left all alone
Adopted by the streets I found my way
Struggling to stay alive day through day
I learned on the streets my way of being a man
In my world I was something people just couldn't understand
In my world people faded in and out
I trusted no one cause...
No one ever taught me
What trust was about
From the beginning I lived my parent's lies
To make family
Yet, they broke their ties
The mistakes I made in this world fell upon unforgiving hands
I was cast out when I tried to learn the right way
To be a man
I was wrote off and placed to the side
I never cared enough to swallow my pride
There were days I had dry tears of whelps
From screaming so loud on how to receive help
In my world I had to keep my tears and pain
To admit I was scared would've drove me insane
I couldn't be weak in a world I didn't choose
At the start it seems this life I was born to lose
I found strength though in my struggle to survive
The world started to change at that moment in my eyes
The moment I chose to stand up in Christ and rise

8/09/2006

— 114 —

"BELIEVE, ACHIEVE, SUCCEED"

To BELIEVE means to find hope in your life
To ACHIEVE is to take the bad and press on through
To SUCCEED is to go beyond yourself to accomplish your dreams
Believing is hard under the influence
Drugs kill the hope that life brings
Achieving is impossible while trippin
Succeeding can never happen while drugs impair your thoughts
Believe that you can make a change
To achieve your dreams for a brighter life
That you will succeed in being the difference to the world you live in
By believing in your abilities
To achieve your dreams
To succeed in life
While living drug free

Written by
Janae Brown and Carandus Brown

08/17/2006

"A MIRACLE ONCE HAPPENED"

A miracle once happened
That broke down fears
Somebody took on a challenge
That continued over the years
The future of the world began to beam
While people lit up with hope
That someone taught the world to dream
Someone dared to take a chance
To enlighten the mind of someone else
By teaching knowledge your life could be enhanced
Breaking the shackles of ignorance
A miracle once happened
The day someone chose to step up and teach
Believing to make a difference
The world they could reach
Today a teacher is under rated
Forgotten in students over achievements
Sometimes they stand alone
Through complaining attitudes and filthy mouths
Lack of respect
They still teach on
A miracle happened
The day a teacher taught
A miracle could happen within us all

10/12/2006

TO MY FAMILY

My youngest, A young lady now
I have watched over you throughout the years
Praying that you wouldn't fall into my fears
My baby girl, life was meant to be yours
I know I walked you back into the world

My sons, handsome young men
An unfortunate event brought my baby boy back into my arms again
My oldest son, I see you trying, struggling to survive
Go ahead let that cry out to live and stay alive
I got your brother right here at my side
We're cheering you on boasting with pride

My oldest girl, I feel your strength to move on from the pain
Your embrace of me kept away many nights of teary rain
I couldn't be more proud of the woman you became
A lady that struggled from the past she over came

My sis, we never thought this was how it would be
So to answer your question
You gave them GREAT LOVE in respect of me

My mom, I know keeping everyone together was hard on you
Through plenty of hardships you pressed on through
Tears of joy I gather when I check in on you
One of God's greatest gifts was giving me you
I honor my family for all you have been and still going through
God has truly blessed us as a family and carry us through

A message to my family through the spirit of love

3/07/2007

"SAVE OUR CHILDREN"

Here's a thought to inflame the mind
To embrace our children through these scary times
As parents we need to wake up and realize
What our children deal with before their own eyes
An everyday struggle trying to live and survive
If they are ready or not their futures are on the line
In a war were their bodies are dropping at the front line
A corruption of their innocence from growing up to quick
As children of both sexes learn to turn tricks
They sometimes need to fend for themselves all alone
In a world that leaves us to trust them on their own
We need to wake up and realize
That our children need us to stand and rise
Stop believing these simple lies
That we are all doing what we can
While showing our young men how to fail at being a man
Delivering sex to a young girl as her part in becoming a woman
It is time to uncover our heads
We can't deal with the problem without getting out of bed
It's a challenge today to save our children from this certain death
But by doing nothing
The world we fight to leave our children
In the end will be a memory never felt

6/23/07

"FELT"

Last night
I talked with God
About my feelings for you
I asked him if what I felt was true
If you was the one meant for me
That I feel like you and I was destined to be
I became lost in thought
While my universe came to a halt
All I could do is sit there and smile
While my heart began to beat even loud
My hands became heavy
I became sweaty
I couldn't stop thinking of you
All I wanted was to be with you
I discovered new emotions within myself
That led me to know I didn't want anyone else
God answered me through the way I felt
That there was no doubt left
I knew that this was true
Cause the only one on my mind is you

07/04/2007

"LAST BREATH"

I never thought I would leave this way
I never thought it would be this day
I thought I had more time left
In this life that I was dealt
Being born into hell
When life got started off it failed
My life is filled with ups and downs
It rains so much I'm starting to drown
In the last moment of my last breath
I wasted life in a dead health
Yet God still loved me
Cause before I took it
He forgave me
He reached out his arms
To save me
Pulled me up from that pool of sin I filled
That in my last breath I could live to do his will

8/02/07

"TO KNOW YOU"

I'm not trying to play a game
I just wanted to know your name
Since the day you caught my eye
That night fireworks lit the sky
When I heard you called, I was at a loss of words
You had my nerves all disturbed
Thinking of you now consumes my mind
So, I'm leaving the bull behind
My instincts realize something about you
Now I want to find out if it is true
However, we turn out, rather something more or just friend
Remain in our hands
No surprises or tricks up my sleeve
Just this chance I plan to achieve
To know who it is that intrigues me
That God has presented in front of me
That breaks my thoughts from reality
That has me caught in her attention
So, this my solution
With nothing to hide
I just want you by my side
That I found something in you
That has me craving to know you
Putting away childish things and all nonsense to the left
I am coming at you like there's no one else
EXIST!!!

10/10/2007

"MOST LOVED"

Throughout time I have always loved you
In the past when I was young, I dreamed
Dreams of you
That in the present you are the greatest gift God given to me
My most loved you and my future will forever be
I will never forget what you are to me
You're the twinkle in my eye
When tears of joy flow free
My moment of perfection that was granted to me
My most loved you will always be
Your touch I will always feel in the distant breeze
Your voice I will hear in the echoing trees
Your fragrance I will take in
The way spring come alive
My most loved your persona uplifts me in the beauty of the day
My heart may quit beating one day, but from you it will never die
You are cherished as angels dancing in the sky
Your name will never fall away from my lips
My most loved I will know you from the moment we share our first kiss
My essence of this life will forever belong to you
No other woman will ever hold the meaning you are to me
My vows I will make to you will never leave my soul
My most loved my last breath will always be yours
I will conquer the world till I find you
My faith in God will show the path through
You have my heart, my soul, and my life to bare
That somewhere in time is our moment we share
We are joined as one
My love became yours and....
You became my most loved

4/18/2008

"THE BLESSINGS OF YOU ALL"

This is something that has to be said
You have all become part of the meal that influence the way I am fed
Struggling with a hopeless mentality left over from a young ghetto thug
I learned to embrace who I once was, an education God's way of blessing
me with a hug
Drowning in thoughts of being a bottomless nothing
To being inspired in becoming God's incredible something
Always alone I felt bound and trapped
To be in class with three gifted brothers I know my time has not elapsed
My mind was thrown into an unlocked cage
That I could not open due to an unwritten page
Eye's wide open has me hungry for knowledge released in rage
I found something new that has me becoming
Inspired by a professor that see in me a great leader is now the drive
towards my homecoming
An education once wasted and the fight for knowledge is now confirming
Even though I don't have a plan yet laid out before me
It's through the encouragement of ten amazing women God has shared
with me
No longer lonely or a broken stem with thorns
Amongst all of you I am planted with roses a gift of being reborn
Like a confused insect I was lost to find my place
Through all of you God has shown me his mercy and grace
Truth is I didn't really think I could follow it through
But God's hands are at work within me from the blessings of all of you
Sweat, blood, and tears will be the work that paves my way
But it will be in the blessing of you all
I will obtain my master's degree on **GRADUATION DAY**

11/18/2008

"A MAN BORN TOO EARLY"

Listen as I try to explain me
I was born a man too soon a decade too early
In her womb I was fed life of the streets
Cuz I was born with concrete beneath my feet
Her hopes and dreams must have been diluted from the world she sees
As the streets took my childhood away from me
Wondering why I am the way I am
Knowing this life I live is a sham
As this child try to breathe who I am
Listen as I try to explain
All I ever knew is this ghetto pain
Rotted corpses of breathing bodies make the ghetto a living cemetery
This has been my vision of life since the start of elementary
I was born a man too soon too early
No excuses
This was the life I was dealt
Asking am I an animal for the rage I have felt
Maybe so when all I see is a cage in my face
But living in the ghetto is not my disgrace
The lack of opportunity, the fight to survive in this struggle
I wonder what you would say when I hear your rebuttal
Listen as I try to explain
Unless you lived it you will never truly understand
Why I am the way I am
A man born too soon too early
Breathes a child still making decisions for me

3/25/10

"I'D BE THAT BOYFRIEND"

I'd be your umbrella on rainy
dayz
Your comforter with a warm
embrace
I'd be the man to pull you close
as you tug away
I'd give you that Kiss upon your
lovely face
That at your worst your beauty
still carries thru
In the tears you Shed I will
share your pain
I'd be that man to say I LUV you
Give you a hug to fill you with
the love we gained
If you need to Smile, giggle,
and LAUGH
If you find yourself Gazing
within my eye's
I'd be that man your better half
I will give you my WORLD as I
gaze in your eye's
Lend you an ear when you need to
vent
When you are quiet I will
understand
I'd be that Man a friend that
God has Sent
when you NEED help I will hold
out my hand

when you're scared I will
protect you within my Arms
If you have doubts of who I AM
That I'm the man to keep you
from HURT and harm
I'd be the REAL boyfriend to
reassure you I AM who I AM.

06/22/2010

WHAT COMPLETED ME

It's like I remember us from a time before
A time forbidding to us
Till now forbidding is no more
Time has given us another chance to cherish
I'm taking it by asking you for your hand in marriage
From the first day we met upon eharmony
Something about you took grasp of me and struck me
That in my soul I knew this was destiny
I began falling in love and in fact I fell in love
Instantly I knew God created us from above
I gave you my heart
Together we made a whole part
I was your better half and you were mine
I knew we would be forever till the end of time
I finally knew what completed me
The other living half of me
Now I'm sitting here daydreaming of you
Realizing that my heart now belongs to you
Two souls connecting across the distance of space
Lost in a moment of God's loving grace
From running a weary race
But we made it to win 1st place
I know you are the last woman to enter my life
I know cuz.....
God said Carandus come meet your WIFE
That moment I fell and bowed
That in this poem
I promise you these VOWS!

02/14/2012

"MY VOW"

As I began to think about my vows
I am reminded of a promise God has allowed
To find the meaning of his love
That my vows are a promise to keep God's words
A promise to love you the rest of my days
A promise to cherish you in every way
A promise to be faithful for life
A promise to respect you as my wife
A promise to keep God first
A promise to always make you a part of my world
A promise that each day I will place a smile upon your lovely face
A promise I will forever embrace
That you will remain the sparkle in my eye
Till my last breath I will release it in a cry
A promise made in the presence of God
To share with you a love formed from God's own heart
A promise to understand that I must seek out through God
What God has formed together no one can tear it apart
A promise to be
The best of friends
A promise this as my vow to you
A promise to always be true
To give my all
Is my promise to you

06/11/2013

"A WOMAN OF NOBLE CHARACTER"

A Testament To *Proverbs 31;10-31*

10 A woman of noble character who shall find

He who finds a wife finds what is good and receives favor from the Lord

That James L Walker found in you the strength, love, and endurance of the ties that bind

The foundation to build a strong family embrace

11 Believing God's word that you lack nothing of value

Since day one in the womb, 100 years of his creation God bestowed to us your grace

12 She brings him good, not harm all the days of her life

That as a child I remember attending your 50th anniversary

The strength, dedication, and commitment to be a loving wife

A woman of noble character is the legacy you share to inspire

13 She works with eager hands to provide for her family

I see it every day in my mother, aunts, sisters, daughters, nieces, and female relatives

What my grandfather found in you they admire

17 She sets about her work vigorously; her arms are strong for task

That you carried the world we knew in your arms

A strong black woman He sent in you to fulfill destiny and not lack

20 She open her arms to the poor and extends her hands to care for the needy

That the best in us is because the love you taught and shared in us

To cherish all life and do what we can; instead of falling into greed

25 The woman of noble character is clothed with strength and dignity; that she can laugh at the days to come

Remembering stories family will share on how you held the family strong through difficult times, while keeping happiness around

A proud legacy to teach our girls about who they come from

28 Her children arise and call her blessed; her husband also and he praises her

The angels in heaven praise your works

And we thank you for the woman on earth you were

29 Many women do noble things, but you surpass them all

30 For the women who fears the Lord is to be Praised

As she follows and honors God's call

31 Honor her for all that her hands have done and let her works bring her praise at the city gate

And as you stand in front of God, we stand and praise you as God say;

"Well Done My Good and Faithfull Servant"

Love you Grandma

01/20/2016

"LEGACY"
(A Dedication to Tom McNamara)

Time remembers legacy as what was left behind
Often forgotten is the greatness of a legacy is only found in what's done in the presence of time
A person's true character is discovered in their resolve to tackle adversity
That I remember as a kid hearing the strides your father was fighting in the city
Diversely different and raised in poverty I learned from his legacy Rockford was not a city in pity
Taught that the pride we hold is in the legacy we share
Now your stride to fight is a fight with you we bare
Great leaders have shown that time will heal all wounds in what is done to build your legacy
It will overcome any obstacle, demolish any barrier to bring opportunity in any tragedy
An opportunity to overcome and demolish the fear of what is not yet realized
That even in division and high crime, Rockford's legacy will be a city triumphantly chose to rise
In this presence, your passion to propel your legacy at this moment in time
To bring growth and development in helping the city to continue to brightly shine
That a city in failure or wallowing into a ghost town is not how Rockford will be defined
Like lions the one that roars the loudest victory shall be gained
But it is in the heart to bring together that this city will remain
From the exit of one great leader and through challenges of many other great candidates
It is who you are and who your father was your legacy is being created
That time will remember your legacy in what is done in the presence of time
Never forgotten will be the greatness you choose to leave behind

02/01/2017

THE BLACK WOMAN

The black woman
Often beaten and broken
A sexual side piece used to the bone
Striped down as a slave driven token
Killing her spirit till her soul is gone
Disrespected and ridiculed for being the woman you are
A mother, sister, wife and daughter
A black woman with a past full of scars
Still going to prayer for those she loves at the alter
As a man weakness is to encage her beauty and essence
Through the betrayal of love left her unprotected
God's gift to the world is our need for her presence
The strength of a black woman will never be affected
Engraved in the color of her skin is more than enough
That the world shall finally know her worth
Because deep is her greatness the world has only scuffed
In the start of creation God chose the black woman to be its birth
So rise black woman, stand up and rise
Let your voice of who you are speak out loud
You will never fall from a past of hurt and lies
In the end the black woman will reign true and proud

Written by Jamaia Brown and Carandus Brown Sr.

02/22/2017

I DON'T KNOW

I don't know the equation of time
To tell how long it takes to heal the tears we have
Listening to the silence in a quiet sign
That at this moment is all we have
I don't know that this is the end of the road
How long it takes to bring comfort to your soul
But I'm grateful for the mother's love you showed
That in this difference I am now whole
I don't know how to change things around
How one moment has dealt a blow of pain
But keep me as the joyous thoughts of love found
That from birth you taught the world has gained
I don't know if destiny is true to design
How to give back that moment lost
That I am solving the equation of time
Repaving a brand-new road
Changing the world around
To make destiny fit in your design
I don't know is what I prove to know

04/07/2017

"MY BELOVED SON"

My Beloved Son
A message to my First Born
In our hearts you are still adored
In our life your spirit sored
Missed by your father, brother, sister, friends, and all
That in this moment time has paused
Teaching to love life and the fulfillment to rise
That your nephews learned to become men through your eyes
Remembering the Jokester with the soul of laughter
Sharing pure enjoyment even after
Reminiscing a proud true cowboy fan through thick and thin
In sad times you still bring happiness from within
My beloved son
This is my message to my first born
You lived life as your name foretold you to be
Absolute **D**istinct **A**ttributes **M**ade **R**eady **O**n **S**erving **S**ignificantly
Even your nickname showed rule
You were respected because you gave your best to the kids in school
Called A – Ross Tha Boss
This world has been dealt a great loss
A message to my first born
My dear and beloved son

11/17/2017

A HUG AND A SMILE

In the sense of care
You had the biggest heart
Greeted with a hug and a smile you loved to share
That the days are heavy, dim, and flat
Knowing you not here to give your part
But remembering you keeps the light shining
As we would say Hi, I will miss the small chat
Being touched with perfect affection at the right timing
A lady of divine grace
Cherished and honored a loving friend
Missing you as the world is now a smaller place
A hole in space a bigger void in the world
To fill your words of encouragement that only you could send
You taught lessons of gratitude to sometimes an undeserving world
That I will truly miss the person you have shown
The commitment to people and the dedication to care
That it will always be your hug and smile
I will remember and share

10/20/2017

A FATHER'S PRIDE

You might have been too young to know
The hard part was not having the moment to say goodbye
But my blessing has been in the moments of watching you grow
In certain glances, I was right by your side
Holding you in your moment of need
You are the pride a father prays and hope for
A young lady drove to succeed
While struggling over identity to find so much more
God's gift is that I share tears of joy on sunny days of rain
Watching over you is a Father's pride
As you grow to be the woman of fain
Prepare for life, ups and downs as a steep climb or a slippery slide
Granted moments of joy to help guide you in your growth
As Angels share my notes of comfort in moments of loneliness
A Father's pride to see you accomplish your dreams is my oath
In spirit with you in oneness
And
If you were too young to know
Each and every moment is cherished in watching you grow

Dedicated to Sierra Christina Jacobs
"In Loving Memory of her Father"

07/22/2018

"SALVATION"

A choice for life to save sinful people at the point of His death
Knowing the knowledge, He is who we cannot see
Imagine that moment of His crucifixion
Feel the sadness and agony as he took his last breath
As the tears of a mother were being shed to see her son die
And
The Father still giving His love in the presence of that dark moment
It is a gift of salvation through the hate of His crucifixion
Now feel the anger and pain the people had, slash
after slash, as the beating began
Listen to the crowd shout, "Kill Him" with laughter
as they proudly boast in their sin
He offered Salvation, as they rioted in the fame to kill His son
That selfish people may live with Him the way creation began
Think about that moment as he was nailed to the cross
Hear Him as He ask, "Father forgive them
for they know not what they do"
Salvation for all, as people thought they had cursed Him to the grave
That after His death, three days He was raised
Power, commitment, and love is what He gave
An everlasting sacrifice for a people with selfish ways.
A price of salvation offered freely over death is what He paid
That you will know Salvation is a choice for your life
Jesus was crucified on an unending day
That you either continue to crucify him or you
believe to walk that path with him
Salvation is to touch His spirit and be anointed with the power
To help the world find their place in the kingdom of heaven

11/09/2018

"THE WORLD CAN BE A BOOK"

We can be like the greatest book ever read
Or
The greatest story ever told
A multitude of volumes, where diversity is led
Many different cultures
and
Many different chapters
Time cannot be held in life but, in a book, time is on hold
Plenty of minutes in a day
and
Plenty of letters on a page
A different person met, a different persona of characters
We can be as many great genres to behold and engage
A family in life, a family of words
Linked to bring together or to tell a tale
Drama and tragic plots, life's negative events that are blurred
A plot of inspiration full of details and motivation
Creating joy in giving new life
Set in the midst of a furious devastation
A new scheme to pick apart or derail
We can be a world writing a new beginning
The greatest author's assembling the tools to deliver a masterpiece
Connecting with hope, faith, and love in a novel never ending
We can be the reader to open the cover and seek what lies beneath
The world can be a book if reading it is your option

03/12/2019

"THE GREATEST LOVE STORY LEFT UNTOLD"

Destiny has a way of grabbing a hold to you
Telling what's real, fake, the lies and what's true
Creating moments that shatters all fragments of reality
Piecing together a thread of what could be actually
Shared by two in another life or a dream
That destiny speaks loud for what it brings
My mind with you plus body and soul
To share the greatest love story left untold
In my world you were the one that got a way
A space in time that lost its day
But my thoughts are like harmony of what we shared
As brief as it was, still my heart, I bared
If immature thoughts would have heard what destiny said
My love could have been fed
Instead, an apology of words that's a slur
But I'm thankful for you for being the lady you were
A friend with true intentions for the world to hold
That I share with you my greatest love story left untold.

10/20/2019

"APPRECIATED PART 2"

Through the short time
I have known you, you've been
A guide, a teacher, a straightforward leader, and a spiritual friend
The best in you seek the best in us
which is found to be rare in people today
And I appreciate you, for all that you do
I can say I have grown
In this short-time, I spent learning under you
I appreciate the knowledge giving freely
And the hard work and dedication you to bestowed in us
That we appreciate you, for all that you do
Gifted by God to share with us all
Rebuilding a team that we may not fall
Sharing that care
As one unit growing together
Now that we are here with more growing to do
we are stronger now
And that's why I appreciate you

04/01/2019

THE LEADER IN YOU

(Dedicated to Mrs. Laura Synder)

I can see the leader in you
Building bridges of hope
To overcome that obstacles of poverty that many construe
A leader climbing destiny's slippery slope
That there are moments in life that is led by destiny
Then there are those moments that destiny is driven
Through your hard work and dedication, God has given you an epiphany
To lead a vision where much must be given
In moments that you can seem dark and alone
It is your courage to stand in front of the opposition
That guide your steps, when peace appears to be gone
God has placed you as that leader and granted you commission
It's not always easy to lead with authority those that cannot hear your voice
In some moments, chaos may seem to be in control from the far back perspective
That through your perseverance in making difficult decisions will provide the right choice
The overall vision to believe in attaining the objective
A straightforward and transparent leader in guiding in an open way
I believe in the leader in you
Because in difficult moments it's the leader that bring clarity to the start of each day
That barriers of poverty are torn down and is no longer construed

06/30/2019

THE MEASURES OF A MAN
(Dedicated to Ron Clewer)

As character builds the measures of a man
Life choices determines his destiny in the grasp of his hand
His struggles dealt from of young
Measures the heart of courage in a battle he's destined to overcome
The measure of a man stands tall in the midst of adversity
To bring justice in the reckoning of an unbalanced diversity
His measures lead the good fight, disliked by many
To find those on his side leaping off by the plenty
The measures of a man carry out what's right
Even if it cost him to lose friends overnight
He stands alone in his goals to bring compassion
In this, his dedication to fulfill his measures overflows his ration
The measures of a man to lead the just cause
Breaking the silence of the wrongs of the past once held on pause
A man measured by God chose to be great amongst many but bestowed
in only a few
He follows God's will in his actions and his path he triumphs through
He faces the challenges of life head on to teach character to others
Even if his character is questioned and tested by his brothers
To guide his family through his conflictions
Measures his motivation from his convictions
In his choices to do right, he refuses to sit out
Believing in his measures to overcome all doubts
You will never understand his thoughts by the decisions he makes
His ideas are not for his glory but for the world we make
Guiding his destiny, his measures gripped tightly in the palm of his hand
In his legacy, reveals the measures of a great destined man

07/13/2019

"THE TRUTH IN A VISION"
(Dedicated to **Multimedia Marketing Group**)

Some see what they want, while others have visions of what could be
The vision to lead and change a perspective of reality
The ability to think about or plan the future with imagination or wisdom
A Multimedia Marketing approach to overcome a broken system
Can the world be changed from what is viewed?
In a lapse of judgmental thoughts twisted to misconstrue
Found the perfect concept to pinpoint a better future
Born a Multimedia Marketing trend based on wisdom to lead a different culture
All I hear and see in the world of media
A never-ending account of human failure's, a cyclopedia
Devastation, hate, anger, and tragedy
Multimedia Marketing makes a creative way of thinking rationally
A fresh start to heal an old broken design
A God driven vision guided from the frontline
Today's media is not all in decay
But through unfavorable news facts, its decomposing day by day
It takes a special heart to challenge the status quo
To plan and implement higher standards to change the view of what we know
Multimedia Marketing implores for a better world to be received
Their Vision is given clear, ready, and achieved

08/01/2019

"YOUNG, BLACK, AND TROUBLED"

Here's a thought to provoke a discussion
To the mind not already set in erosion
What do you see when you look at me?
Could it be the Joy of poverty bestowed upon this life for the world to see!
Or the pure delight in the pain our ancestors fought to free
An injustice to justice for walking in the shoes of a lost forgotten black man
You expect me to be happy, but I'm Angry and Disturb from a constant fight with unhealed hands
This is the life I live on broken knees, I stand
Everyday a different battle, everyday it seems to double
Yet, you will only see that I'm Young, Black, and Troubled
As parents it was never intended for us to grow up this way
The hopeless discarded dreams of a mother's fight to just make it to another day
Encouragement is what was hoped would pave the way
Inside at one point there was a good soul
Corruption crept in and dug its hole
A cracked smile pretending to hide inner tears
Shattered courage covering the wall of fears
A confused cry for help beneath a bunch of misunderstood messages in a pile of rubble
Yet, all you see is that I'm Young, Black, and Troubled
I will never be the person your society say I need to be
But I'm more than Young, Black, and Troubled because God is leading me
With the potential to rise above your decapitating vision
If you take the chance to see what's inside me as your decision!

08/12/2019

"LIVE LIKE GREAT MEN"
(Dedicated to Marcus Hill)

Let me tell you what I see
A blessed life of a great man
Like MLK you fight the good fight
Sharing your knowledge for your people to be free
The legacy to live like a great man
In God's hand He gifted your sight
Like Moses leading into the promise land
Like Jacob becoming Israel, you wrestled with God for your blessing
As Abraham walked and talked with God, in front of your family strong
you stand
Like Malcolm X, "by any means necessary" overcoming the odds has been
your life's lesson
This is what I Know
Like David, you have a heart after God's own
To battle giants fearlessly with the courage of God you show
Like Daniel in the Lion's den you face adversity strong
Like John the baptize, you prepare the way
Like Isiah, your vision guides restoration of greatness
As Matthew, Mark, Luke, and John you share the word for people to weigh
Like Solomon, requesting wisdom over wealth in the fullness
Let me tell you what I admire
Like Jonah you rebelled to come back to the truth
Like Abimelech, Meshach, and Abednego standing for what's right into the
burning flame you choose
Like Saul conversion to Paul God used your past that His light you would
produce
A life lived like a strong black man you strive to aspire
Like Job you have the faith to remain joyful in dealing with the darkest news
That through God you lived like Great Men the trust He bestowed in You

02/28/2020

"GOD'S VESSEL"
(Dedicated to Dwight Clark)

You are God's vessel in the thick of confusion
His voice to speak clarity in times of disillusion
Not many people allow God to use them
But you are that one who choose not to doubt him
You are God's vessel when the world is in doubt
An honest man following Jesus route
God is blessing you through your choices to live in truth
A guided spirit bestowed in the things you do
He sees the man that you have become
Inspiring others to strive in their full potential to overcome
Every obstacle designed to tear them down
You are God's vessel, when people need him around
His words bring life through you in the hour of need
You are God's vessel taking time in others to water His seed
Life has choices, full of positive and negative decisive decision
That's why God has you as his living vessel in times of confusion

04/10/2020

ABOUT THE AUTHOR

Carandus Brown is a devoted man to true Christian principles with hopes to encourage people to find Jesus for themselves. He is a loving husband and blessed father of seven children (6 daughters and 1 son). Carandus is a Minister of the gospel and use his poetry as a teaching method in allowing the Holy Spirit to flow freely. He continues to write uplifting and inspirational poems as the Holy spirit reveals life's stories.

Printed in the United States
By Bookmasters